TIMELINES FROM BLACK HISTORY

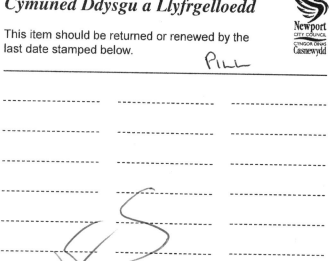

TIMELINES FROM BLACK HISTORY

Leaders, Legends, Legacies

DK LONDON
Designer Joe Lawrence
Senior Editor Steven Carton
Illustrator Lauren Quinn
DK Media Archive Romaine Werblow
Picture Researchers Rituraj Singh, Vagisha Pushp
Managing Editor Lisa Gillespie
Managing Art Editor Owen Peyton Jones
Production Editor George Nimmo
Senior Production Controller Rachel Ng
Jacket Designer Surabhi Wadhwa-Gandhi
Jackets Design Development Manager Sophia MTT
Publisher Andrew Macintyre
Art Director Karen Self
Associate Publishing Director Liz Wheeler
Publishing Director Jonathan Metcalf
Writer and consultant Mireille Harper

DK DELHI
Senior Jacket Designer Suhita Dharamjit
Senior DTP Designer Harish Aggarwal

First published in Great Britain in 2020 by
Dorling Kindersley Limited
DK, One Embassy Gardens, 8 Viaduct Gardens,
London, SW11 7BW

Copyright © 2020 Dorling Kindersley Limited
A Penguin Random House Company
10 9 8 7 6 5 4 3 2 1
001–323546–October/2020

A CIP catalogue record for this book
is available from the British Library.
ISBN: 978-0-2415-0361-4

Printed and bound in the UK

For the curious
www.dk.com

This book was made with Forest Stewardship Council ™
certified paper – one small step in DK's commitment
to a sustainable future.
For more information go to www.dk.com/our-green-pledge

MIX
Paper from
responsible sources
FSC™ C018179

Content from previous books

Roughly two-thirds of the content in this book has been published before in the DK books *Timelines of Everything* (2018) and *Timelines of Everyone* (2020). This material has been updated with new stories and images to more fully reflect Black history. We decided to gather it together with some wonderful new content in order to focus on Black history and Black people. We did this to more fully reflect the identities, cultures, contributions, and experiences of people of Black and mixed heritages throughout history and around the world.

Focusing on Black history

Traditionally, history has been recorded and written by men from privileged backgrounds, who often have a European focus when they assess the past. This has meant that most history books have hidden, overshadowed, and excluded the exciting lives and amazing accomplishments of women, and of people from different ethnic and cultural backgrounds. We've made this book differently: here you will find wonderful timelines that focus on amazing Black history, and amazing Black people of different genders, nationalities, beliefs, heritages, religions, and sexualities.

Travelling through time

Some dates have BCE and CE after them. These are short for "before the Common Era" and "Common Era". The Common Era dates from when people think Jesus Christ was born.

Where the exact date of an event is not known, "c." is used. This is short for the Latin word circa, meaning "around", and indicates that the date is approximate.

When an event in a timeline carries on for more than one year, we have used "..." to indicate this – for example, "1983..." means this event started in 1983 and carried on for a while after.

CONTENTS

Foreword

As a young child, my mum would tell me stories about brilliant Black people throughout history. My favourite was Nanny of the Maroons, a national hero in Jamaica, where my mum was born. Nanny was the leader of a community of formerly enslaved people known as the Maroons, who she led to victory against British colonizers. She was a real-life heroine. Learning about Nanny and all the revolutionary people that had come before me, I felt inspired and empowered from a young age, and proud of my heritage.

When I started going to school, however, I found that the heroes I knew and loved weren't recognized. My school history books and curriculum often featured only white people, and mentioned Black people only in the context of slavery. I knew that there had been Black leaders, historians, activists, writers, politicians, and changemakers – so why weren't they celebrated, too?

Black history has been overlooked and minimized in every area of society, and even worse, often erased. Yet, the contributions of Black people to society influence every part of how we live, from the art and culture we consume, to the rights we have. At the time of writing this, one of the biggest global movements in history, Black Lives Matter, has shone a light on the injustices that still exist in society. At a time when Black people are continuing to face racism, hostility, and discrimination, it is more vital than ever that our history is celebrated.

Over the course of this book, you will meet a plethora of inspirational and influential names throughout history. Spanning the UK, the US, Africa, the Caribbean, and beyond, and covering the mighty African empires, the Colonization of Africa, the US Civil Rights Movement and more, you'll learn about some of the most defining periods in history, and the people who paved the way for others to follow – from the literary legend Maya Angelou and the incredible environmentalist Wangari Maathai, to the luminaries of this generation, such as the British rapper Stormzy, and activists Amariyanna Copeny and Marley Dias. My hope is that the legends, leaders, and legacies in this book speak to you just like the stories from my youth spoke to me.

Mireille Harper

Black culture, contributions, and consciousness – they are the past, the present, and the future.

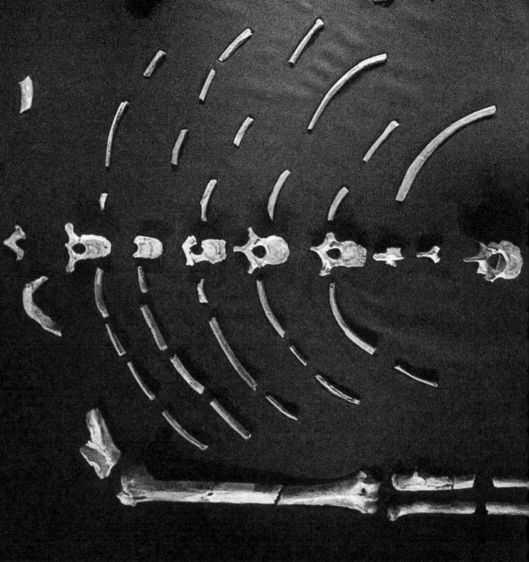

Lucy

In 1974, anthropologists discovered parts of a fossilized skeleton while digging in Ethiopia. They named the *Australopithecus afarensis* skeleton Lucy, and later analysis showed that Lucy lived about 3.2 million years ago, making her the oldest human ancestor found at that time. Several hundred pieces of fossilized bone found make up about 40 per cent of Lucy's skeleton.

c.65 MYA...   **c.5.8 MYA...**   **c.4 MYA...**   **c.2.5 MYA...**   **c.1.9 MYA...**   **c.1.5 MYA...**

Primates

The earliest human ancestors we know about are primate-like mammals. They have small bodies and look similar to modern monkeys and apes. Over time, these animals evolve and divide into two groups: one which leads to gorillas, and the other to hominins (human-like primates).

Australopithecus

Primate ancestors of humans, known as *Australopithecus*, live in various places in Africa. They walk on two legs and have small canine teeth, just like modern humans. Millions of years later in 1974, anthropologists in Ethiopia find a fossil-like skeleton from the era, which they name Lucy.

Homo erectus

Facing difficult weather and living conditions, some early human species known as *Homo erectus* ("upright human") migrate out of Africa, eventually reaching as far as modern-day Southeast Asia. They are the first hominin with the body size of modern humans.

Fire

Early signs of human ancestors using fire are found in Koobi Fora and Chesowanja, Kenya. Areas of reddened soil and stone tools date back to about 1.5 million years ago: evidence that fire is used in the process of cooking food.

Orrorin tugensis

One of the earliest-known hominins, *Orrorin tugenensis* has human-like traits such as walking upright, but climbs trees and has ape-like teeth.

Homo habilis

Primates known as *Homo habilis* live across sub-Saharan Africa. They have larger brains and more human-like features – so much so that they are considered to be the first proper human ancestors. Nicknamed "handy human", *Homo habilis* make stone tools, often for cutting and chopping meat, a staple of their diet.

GUIDE SHOWING FRAGMENTS OF FOSSILS AT KOOBI FORA

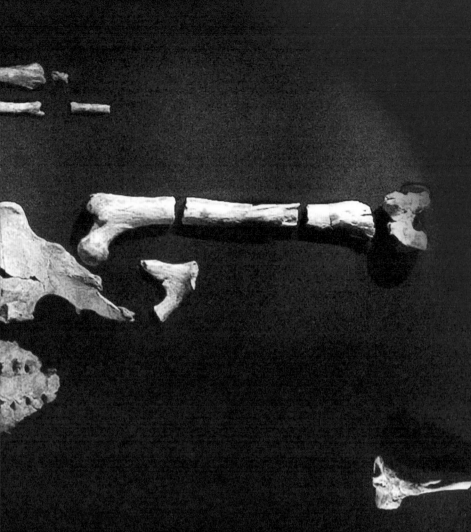

African origins

Evolution is the slow process of living things changing over millions of years. The fossil record shows that our species, *Homo sapiens*, began as *Homo habilis*, about 2.5 million years ago (MYA). It also shows that the entire human story began in Africa, with our ancestors gradually spreading out across Earth.

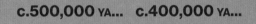

c.500,000 YA...   **c.400,000 YA...**   **c.200,000 YA...**   **c.200,000– 150,000 YA...**   **c.400 YA...**

Shelter
Homo erectus living in parts of Asia build shelters. In 2001, the oldest structure is found in Tokyo, Japan, by archaeologists, who find stone tools around a hut-like structure.

Homo sapiens
All human beings today belong to the *Homo sapiens* species, which originates in Africa. Some later migrate to Asia, Europe, and the other continents. They have larger brains and lighter skeletons than their ancestors.

First civilizations
Homo sapiens develop speech and writing systems as well as rituals, traditions, and ways of living, all hallmarks of the first civilizations. Today, roughly 1.3 billion people live in Africa, with perhaps a further 220 million people who claim African descent living on other continents.

Homo neanderthalensis
Found across Europe and Asia, the *Homo neanderthalensis* are similar to earlier human species, but have stockier bodies. They are skilled hunter-gatherers, make symbolic ornaments and objects, and overlap with modern humans (*Homo sapiens*), but later become extinct.

STONE HAND AXE MADE BY EARLY *HOMO SAPIENS*

Mitochondrial Eve
In 1987, geneticists find that mitochondrial DNA (genetic information passed from mothers to their offspring) from 147 people links to a common female ancestor, living around 200,000–150,000 years ago. Named Mitochondrial Eve, she is the most-recent common ancestor to all modern humans. She is believed to have lived in modern-day Botswana.

Early African kingdoms

Africa has been home to some of the wealthiest, most powerful, and most culturally fruitful civilizations in world history. Many of these kingdoms left a lasting legacy in art, architecture, religion, and traditions, both within Africa and further afield.

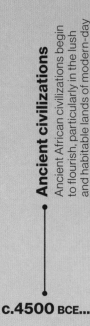

Aksum obelisk

The Aksumite Empire created some highly distinctive architecture. Their carved granite obelisks (tall pillars) are believed to mark the location of the underground tombs of the kingdom's previous rulers. This one stands in the ancient city of Aksum, Ethiopia.

c.4500 BCE...

Ancient civilizations

Ancient African civilizations begin to flourish, particularly in the lush and habitable lands of modern-day Nigeria and Cameroon in West Africa.

c.3300 BCE...

Nubian kingdoms

The region of Nubia (modern-day southern Egypt and northern Sudan) is home to multiple kingdoms that rise and fall from this time. These kingdoms trade in gold, ebony, ivory, and incense, among other goods.

c.2500 BCE...

Punt

Though historians debate its exact location, evidence of the Kingdom of Punt come from records of it trading with Ancient Egypt. Known as the "Land of the Gods", it is vastly rich, with its exports including woods, perfumes, cosmetics, and animals.

c.1730 BCE...

Kingdom of Kush

Located around the Nile River Valley, the Kingdom of Kush controls Nubia in this period. Kush's cities and towns contained distinctive pyramids and temples.

c.1000 BCE...

Farming people

From their homeland in modern-day Nigeria, Bantu-speaking farming people move south and east through Africa. They grow yams, cassava, millet, and sorghum. By 600 BCE, they are also able to make iron tools.

Da'amat

Often cited as the first kingdom in Ethiopia, Daamat is a small but highly sophisticated and literate society. The Temple of Yeha, said to be dedicated to the god Ilmuqah, will survive to be one of the lasting traces of the kingdom. It is the oldest building in modern-day Ethiopia.

c.980 BCE...

Aksumite Empire

Located in the rocky highlands of Ethiopia, the Aksumite Empire is one of the most literate and urbanized states of its time. The Aksumites not only have advanced architecture such as temples and palaces, but also build dams and reservoirs, and trade with Arabia across the Red Sea.

This carved figure of a bull was found in an Ethiopian site connected to the Aksumite Empire. It features inscriptions in Arabic, and is evidence of the trading relationship between the two areas.

c.80 BCE...

First Christian state

When King Ezana of Aksum converts to Christianity, Aksum becomes the world's first Christian state. Coins issued during his reign drop pagan images and begin to show the cross, a symbol of Christianity.

c.400 CE...

Empire of Ghana

The Empire of Ghana becomes the first great West African trading state. Ghana is rich in gold, which it trades with North Africans who cross the Sahara Desert by camel.

c.400...

Kanem-Bornu Empire

The Kanem-Bornu Empire, which stretches from modern-day Chad to southern Libya, begins to flourish. It becomes an Islamic empire in 1085. The empire is on a trade route from the Nile Valley to sub-Saharan Africa.

c.850...

Zimbabwe

The Kingdom of Zimbabwe emerges in southeast Africa. It trades in salt, iron, copper, and ivory. Its capital, known as Great Zimbabwe, features towers that are the largest structures in sub-Saharan Africa before European conquest.

c.1100...

Mali Empire

The Mali Empire conquers Ghana. The capital is Timbuktu, famed for its wealth. In 1324, King Mansa Musa sets off on a two-year pilgrimage to the holy city of Mecca, giving away so much gold along the way that the metal plunges in value.

1324

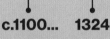

Great Zimbabwe

The ancestors of the modern-day Shona people in southern Africa established the impressive Kingdom of Zimbabwe about 1,000 years ago. At the height of its power, the capital city, Great Zimbabwe, may have been home to more than 18,000 people. At its centre, protected by 11-m (33-ft) tall walls, is the *Imba Huru* (Great Enclosure). It is thought to have housed the royal family and other important people. For years, many non-Africans disputed the achievements of the Kingdom of Zimbabwe – wrongly stating that Black Africans could not have built a society and monuments of this complexity.

Mansa Musa

One of the greatest African rulers of all time, Mansa Musa (1280–1337) led the Mali Empire at the height of its power, wealth, and creativity. During his reign, the empire stretched for 3,200 km (2,000 miles) across West Africa.

Egypt
On Musa's journey, he passes through Cairo in Egypt. To show his peaceful intentions and the incredible wealth of his empire, he gives away so much gold that it causes the value of the precious metal to decrease.

Expanding empire
While Musa is extremely generous on his travels, his trip is also political. He acquires Gao, the capital of the neighbouring Songhai Empire, which is one of the oldest trading centres in West Africa.

Money matters
Mali is rich in natural resources such as gold, precious stones, minerals, and salt. Musa adds to the empire's wealth by introducing taxes on trade and mining, and by taxing conquered neighbouring lands.

Pilgrimage to Mecca
A committed Muslim, Musa makes Islam the official religion of the Mali Empire. In 1324, Musa leaves Mali on the *hajj* – the pilgrimage to the holy city of Mecca that is seen as a spiritual duty of all Muslims.

Becoming Mansa
Musa is appointed deputy to Mansa Abu Bakr II, who embarks on an Atlantic Ocean expedition but never returns. The who gains the throne is passed on to Musa, meaning the title Mansa, becoming the "emperor", becoming the tenth ruler of the Mali Empire.

Born into royalty
Mansa Musa, called Keita at birth, is the great-nephew of the royal Musa Keita of the Mali founder of this royal connection. Musa's father Keita. Despite Musa's did and grandfather Mali. not rule Mali.

1280

1312

1320

1324

July 1324

1325

Mali emperors

The Mali Empire was one of the greatest African empires in history. It was renowned for its wealth and its influence on West African culture.

Sundiata Keita (?–c.1255)

Sundiata Keita was king of the Mandinka people and the first ruler of the Mali Empire, which he established around 1235. He expanded and developed the empire until his death about 1255.

Abu Bakr II (?–c.1312)

The ninth mansa of the Mali Empire, Abu Bakr II was also an avid explorer. He departed from Mali with 200 boats laden with gold and goods in order to "explore the limits of the ocean". He was never seen again.

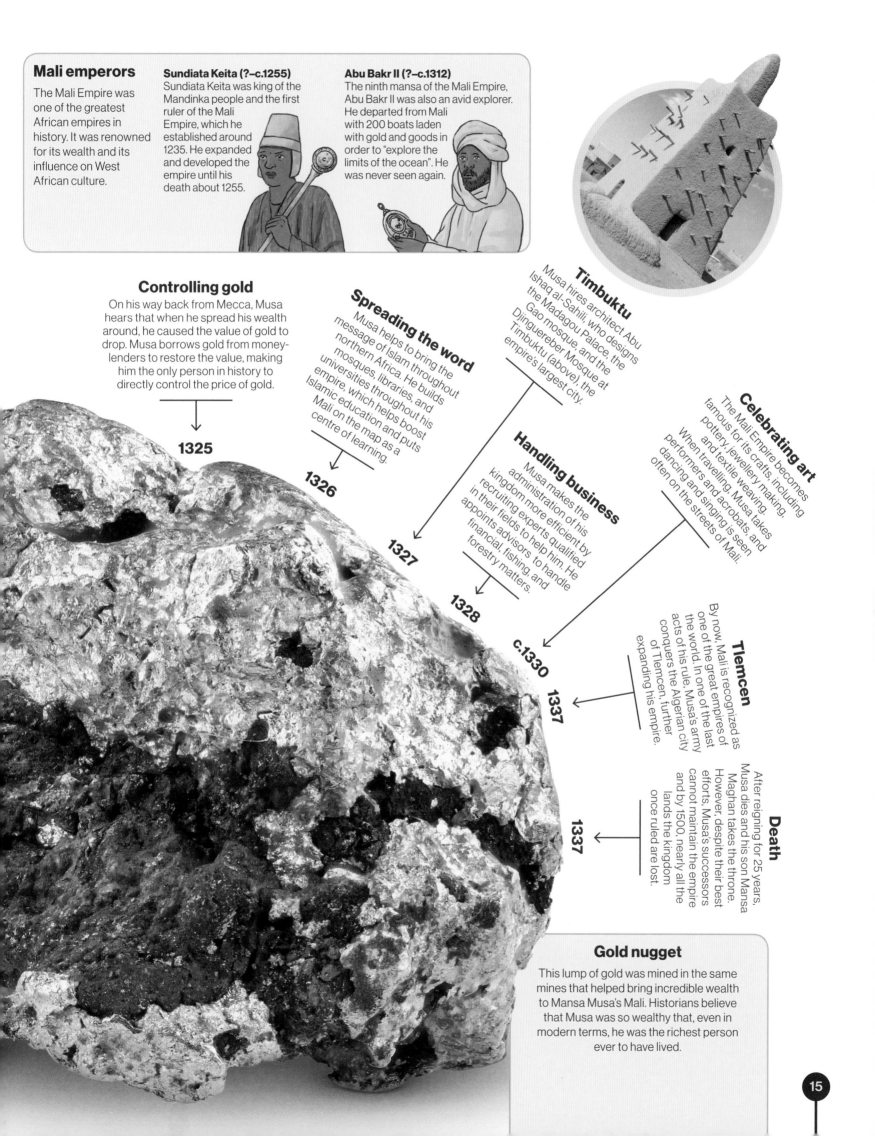

Controlling gold

On his way back from Mecca, Musa hears that when he spread his wealth around, he caused the value of gold to drop. Musa borrows gold from money-lenders to restore the value, making him the only person in history to directly control the price of gold.

1325

Spreading the word

Musa helps to bring the message of Islam throughout northern Africa. He builds mosques, libraries, and universities throughout his empire, which helps boost Islamic education and puts Mali on the map as a centre of learning.

1326

Timbuktu

Musa hires architect Abu Ishaq al-Sahili, who designs the Madagou Palace, the Gao mosque and the Djinguereber Mosque at Timbuktu (above), the empire's largest city.

Handling business

Musa makes the administration of his kingdom more efficient by recruiting experts qualified in their fields to help him. He appoints advisors to handle financial, fishing, and forestry matters.

1327

1328

Celebrating art

The Mali Empire becomes famous for its crafts, including pottery, jewellery making, and textile weaving. When travelling, Musa takes performers and acrobats, and dancing and singing is seen often on the streets of Mali.

c.1330

Tlemcen

By now, Mali is recognized as one of the great empires of the world. In one of the last acts of his rule, Musa's army conquers the Algerian city of Tlemcen, further expanding his empire.

1337

Death

After reigning for 25 years, Musa dies and his son Mansa Maghan takes the throne. However, despite their best efforts, Musa's successors cannot maintain the empire and by 1500, nearly all the lands the kingdom once ruled are lost.

1337

Gold nugget

This lump of gold was mined in the same mines that helped bring incredible wealth to Mansa Musa's Mali. Historians believe that Musa was so wealthy that, even in modern terms, he was the richest person ever to have lived.

Meeting the caliph
On the way to Mecca, he meets the caliph of Egypt (the Muslim ruler of the country). Askia is named the caliph's religious representative in West Africa. He completes his pilgrimage to Mecca.

1497

Returning home
Askia makes the journey back to the Songhai Empire. By completing the hajj he has strengthened his authority. His people accept him as their religious leader.

c.1498

The empire expands
The Songhai Empire expands as Askia conquers neighbouring territory. It covers much of modern-day Mali, Niger, and Senegal. This makes it the largest empire in African history.

1500...

1505

Facing defeat
Askia has captured a large area of territory from surrounding states, but he faces a setback when he attacks Borgu (the border region between modern-day Niger and Nigeria). The campaign fails and Askia has to retreat.

Fall from power
At the age of 80, Askia is nearly blind and unable to rule. His son, Musa, revolts against him, and forces him to abdicate. Askia is banished to an island in the River Niger.

1528

Death
Askia dies aged about 95. He is buried in a mud-brick pyramid in Gao (in modern-day Mali) which is still standing today.

1538

WORSHIPPERS PRAY AT THE MOSQUE AT ASKIA'S TOMB.

Askia and his tomb
We have no confirmed portraits of Askia – this one is based on how rulers of his time and place dressed. His tomb is 17 m (56 ft) high, and is built entirely of mud bricks. The wooden beams give the tomb strength, and allow builders to climb it and carry out repairs.

European pressure

Nzinga Mbandi is born. Her father is the king of the Ndongo people. At this time, European countries are taking people from Africa and transporting them to the Americas to work as slaves. Her father tries his best to keep his people safe.

Raids on Ndongo

Nzinga's father dies, and her brother becomes the king. Portuguese soldiers and raiders have established a fort near Ndongo, and begin raiding and enslaving some of the Ndongo people.

Peace treaty

Nzinga's brother sends her to meet with the Portuguese to negotiate a peace treaty. To show their authority over Nzinga, the Portuguese do not offer her a chair. When the Portugese refuse to get her a chair, her assistant lays down so she can sit on him. . Nzinga negotiates an end to the Portuguese raids in exchange for an agreement to trade with them.

c.1583... **c.1617...** **c.1622**

African rulers

Africa has produced many great leaders with compelling stories that often do not get as much attention as they deserve.

King Ezana of Aksum (c.303–c.350)

Ezana ruled over Aksum (a region made up of parts of modern-day Ethiopia and Eritrea). He converted to Christianity as a child, and Aksum became the first Christian kingdom in Africa as a result. He had numerous stone obelisks made that recorded his achievements.

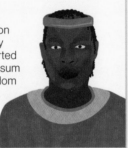

Queen Amina of Zazzau (c.1533–1610)

Queen Amina was a skilled military leader who expanded the city-state of Zazzau (in modern-day Nigeria). To protect Zazzau from its enemies, Amina built huge walls around each of her military camps. Some of these walls are still standing today.

Shaka Zulu (c.1787–1828)

Shaka Zulu emerged as a strong and skilled chief of the Zulu Empire (in modern-day South Africa). Shaka added land from conquered tribes into his empire. He had got on with the European powers in the area, but many of his people grew tired of his rule. He was eventually assassinated by his half-brother.

Nzinga Mbandi

Queen Nzinga Mbandi (c.1583–1663) ruled the kingdoms of Ndongo and Matamba (in modern-day Angola). Mbandi spent most of her reign defending her land from Portuguese colonization, and from raiders trying to enslave her people.

c.1647... **c.1646**

Unlikely allies

Nzinga's forces, along with her Dutch allies, claim a huge victory against the Portuguese. The following year, Portugal calls in reinforcements from their colony in Brazil, and fight back by expelling the Dutch. Nzinga's forces must fight on, without Dutch help.

Warrior queen

With the help of the Imbangala and the Dutch, Nzinga has more of a chance against the Portuguese. Even though she is well past fighting age, Nzinga personally leads her troops into battles.

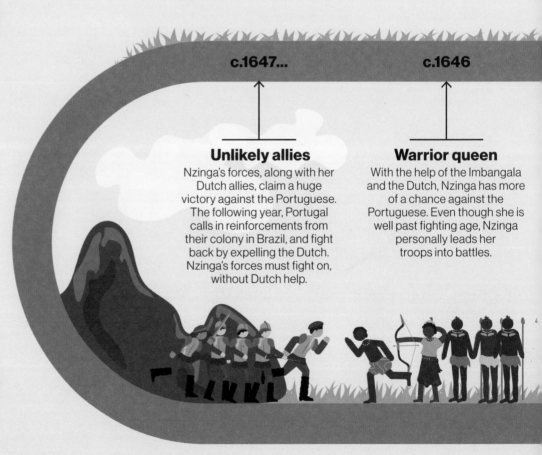

Regent

Nzinga's brother dies. As his heir is too young to rule, Nzinga rules in his place as regent. Some of her tribespeople disagree with this decision.

1624

Becoming queen

The heir to the throne dies, and Nzinga decides to rule herself. Some believe that she had a hand in the heir's death and others feel that a woman should not rule, but she has support from many of her people.

c.1624

c.1626...

Betrayal

The Portuguese break the treaty, and attack Nzinga's people, who are forced to flee Ndongo to the nearby kingdom of Matamba. This marks the beginning of what will be a 30-year war between Nzinga and Portugal.

Dutch alliance

Nzinga allies with the Dutch, Portugal's European rival in the area. Nzinga begins to prepare for an attack on the Portuguese with Dutch help, which she hopes will help her reclaim Ndongo.

1641

Military moves

In Matamba, the Imbangala, a group of African soldiers who had been trained by the Portuguese, join Nzinga. She declares herself the queen of Matamba after conquering the region.

1630

War continues

The back-and-forth war between the Portuguese and Nzinga's forces rumbles on. Though both sides win important victories, neither is able to beat the other completely and to bring the war to an end.

1648...

Peace again

Nzinga's refusal to back down eventually tires the Portuguese armies out. They sign a peace treaty with Nzinga to end the war, and return Ndongo to her. She rules both Ndongo and Matamba until her death in 1663.

1656–1663

Later African kingdoms

In this period, powerful kingdoms and empires continued to rise and fall in Africa. Many of these realms succeeded in trading, in education, and in establishing formidable military forces. However, the arrival of Europeans brought foreign conquest and colonialism to the continent, which changed Africa's story forever.

Songhai Empire

Sonni Ali sets up the Songhai Empire. With his 1468 conquest of Timbuktu, he takes over the Mali Empire and controls trade along the Niger River with a fleet of ships.

c.1464...

GOLD RING OWNED BY AN ASANTE CHIEF

Askia the Great

Askia the Great takes control of the Songhai Empire. His conquests turn the empire into the largest state in West African history. He promotes learning and makes Islam the state religion.

1493...

THE TOMB OF
ASKIA THE GREAT

First European colony

Dutch colonizer Jan van Riebeeck establishes the first European colony at Cape Town in South Africa. This event marks the start of the European colonization of Africa.

1652...

Asante

Consisting of modern-day Ghana, Togo, and Ivory Coast, the Asante Empire is one of the greatest powers in West Africa. It grows rich trading in gold, enslaved people, and guns, and resists European colonization.

c.1670...

Atlantic slave trade

King Charles I of Spain grants a license that allows Africans to be sold as slaves in Spain's American colonies. This leads to a dramatic increase in the number of people enslaved in Africa and forced to work in the Americas – a brutal system known as the Atlantic slave trade.

c.1450...

Benin Empire

Oba (king) Ewuare the Great establishes the Benin Empire. Ewuare conquers 200 neighbouring towns, and also builds a great palace in Benin City.

1440...

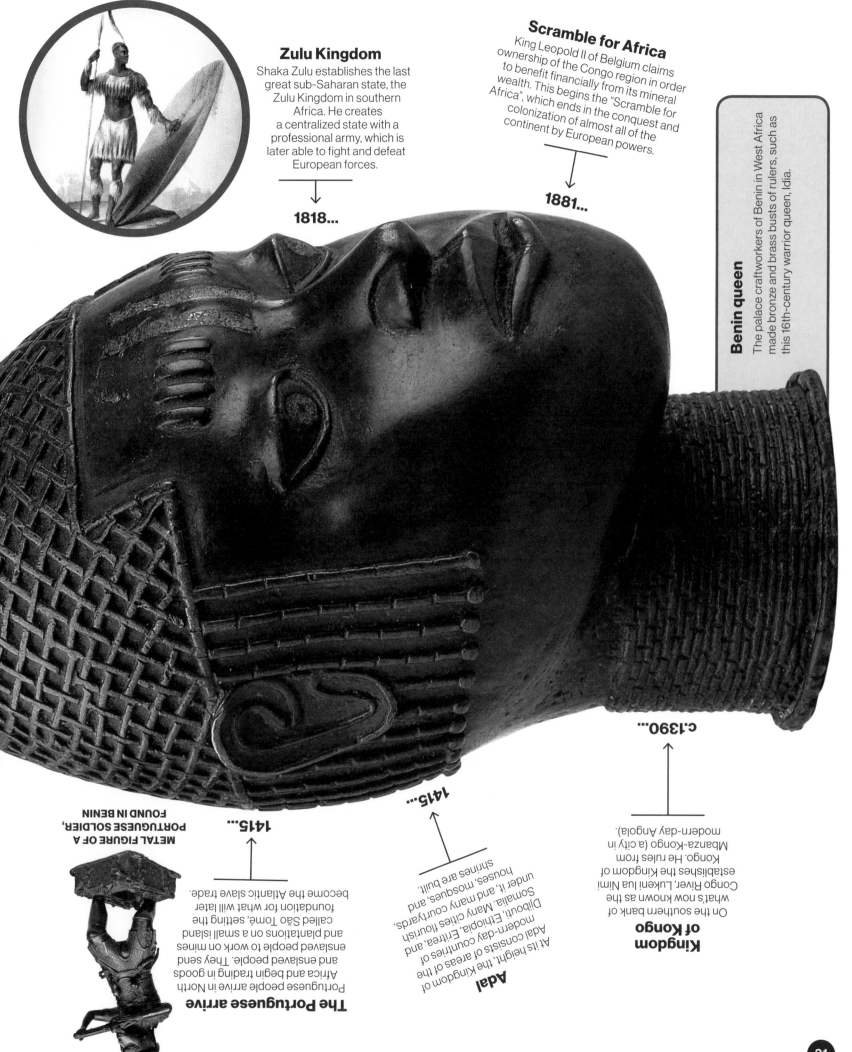

Zulu Kingdom

Shaka Zulu establishes the last great sub-Saharan state, the Zulu Kingdom in southern Africa. He creates a centralized state with a professional army, which is later able to fight and defeat European forces.

1818...

Scramble for Africa

King Leopold II of Belgium claims ownership of the Congo region in order to benefit financially from its mineral wealth. This begins the "Scramble for Africa", which ends in the conquest and colonization of almost all of the continent by European powers.

1881...

Benin queen

The palace craftworkers of Benin in West Africa made bronze and brass busts of rulers, such as this 16th-century warrior queen, Idia.

c.1390....

Kingdom of Kongo

On the southern bank of what's now known as the Congo River, Lukeni lua Nimi establishes the Kingdom of Kongo. He rules from Mbanza-Kongo (a city in modern-day Angola).

1415....

Adal

At its height, the Kingdom of Adal consists of areas of the modern-day countries of Djibouti, Ethiopia, Eritrea, and Somalia. Many cities flourish under it, and many courtyards, houses, mosques, and shrines are built.

1415....

The Portuguese arrive

Portuguese people arrive in North Africa and begin trading in goods and enslaved people. They send enslaved people to work on mines and plantations on a small island called São Tomé, setting the foundation for what will later become the Atlantic slave trade.

METAL FIGURE OF A PORTUGUESE SOLDIER, FOUND IN BENIN

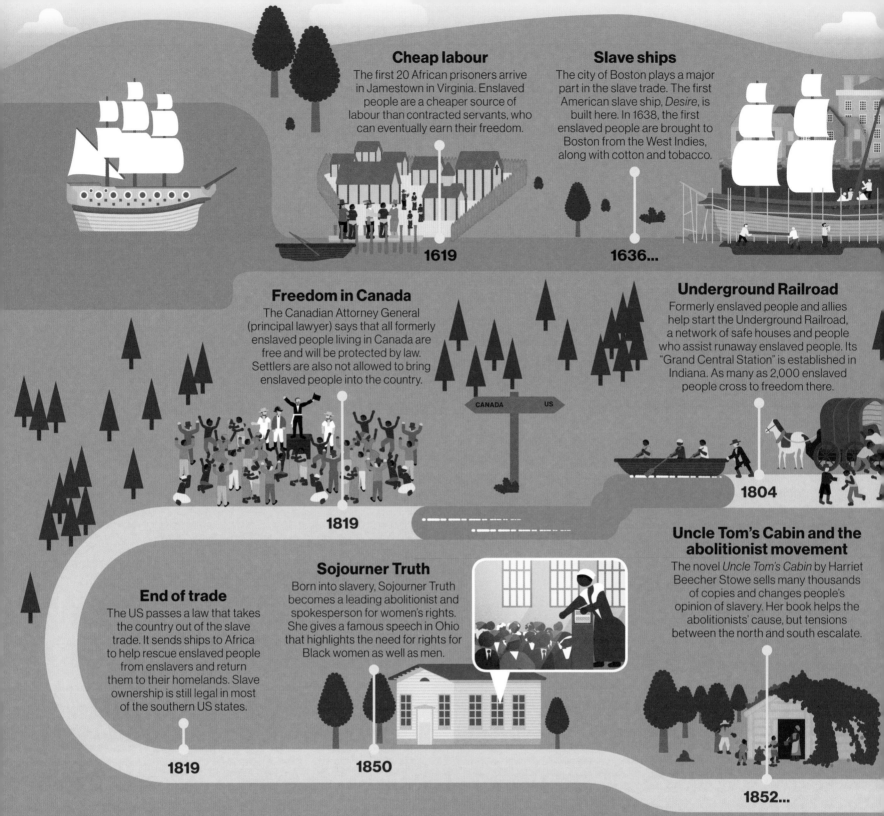

Cheap labour

The first 20 African prisoners arrive in Jamestown in Virginia. Enslaved people are a cheaper source of labour than contracted servants, who can eventually earn their freedom.

1619

Slave ships

The city of Boston plays a major part in the slave trade. The first American slave ship, *Desire*, is built here. In 1638, the first enslaved people are brought to Boston from the West Indies, along with cotton and tobacco.

1636...

Freedom in Canada

The Canadian Attorney General (principal lawyer) says that all formerly enslaved people living in Canada are free and will be protected by law. Settlers are also not allowed to bring enslaved people into the country.

CANADA   US

1819

Underground Railroad

Formerly enslaved people and allies help start the Underground Railroad, a network of safe houses and people who assist runaway enslaved people. Its "Grand Central Station" is established in Indiana. As many as 2,000 enslaved people cross to freedom there.

1804

End of trade

The US passes a law that takes the country out of the slave trade. It sends ships to Africa to help rescue enslaved people from enslavers and return them to their homelands. Slave ownership is still legal in most of the southern US states.

1819

Sojourner Truth

Born into slavery, Sojourner Truth becomes a leading abolitionist and spokesperson for women's rights. She gives a famous speech in Ohio that highlights the need for rights for Black women as well as men.

1850

Uncle Tom's Cabin and the abolitionist movement

The novel *Uncle Tom's Cabin* by Harriet Beecher Stowe sells many thousands of copies and changes people's opinion of slavery. Her book helps the abolitionists' cause, but tensions between the north and south escalate.

1852...

Slavery in the US

Slavery was a brutal part of life in the United States from its colonial beginnings, and enslavers used forced labour to build the young nation and its booming economy. By the 19th century, abolitionists were campaigning to free all slaves, in the face of opposition from many American states. This resulted in civil war, with the north fighting to end slavery, against the south, who wished to retain it.

"**Where any one class is made to feel that society is an organized conspiracy to oppress, rob, and degrade them, neither persons nor property will be safe**".
Frederick Douglass, *from a speech* **(1886)**

A life of slavery

In Virginia, the General Assembly passes a law stating that any child born to an enslaved mother will also become an enslaved person for life. Most slave-holding colonies or states go on to enact similar laws that discriminate by race.

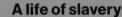

1662

Quaker protest

In Pennsylvania, Quakers protest against slavery. The Quakers are Christians, who believe in treating others fairly. Later, the Quaker Church prevents members from profiting from the slave trade and from owning enslaved people.

1688

Plantations of rice

Rice is introduced in South Carolina. It takes a lot of work to grow it, so European settlers need slave labour to tend the crops and help them make it profitable. By around 1710, there are more enslaved Africans in the state than Europeans.

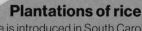

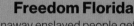

1694...

The life of a slave

The first slave narrative, a story written by a formerly enslaved person about the experience of slavery, is written in New York. Many more narratives follow, one of the most famous of which is written by Frederick Douglass in 1845.

1772...

Freedom Florida

Runaway enslaved people get their freedom in the Spanish territory of Florida. They must give their loyalty to Spain and join the Catholic Church. Many settle in St. Augustine, the oldest European city in the US.

1731

Civil War

The debate over whether or not new states should use enslaved people splits the country in two. Northern victory in this four-year conflict ends slavery, but more than 600,000 people lose their lives.

1861...

Emancipation Proclamation

All enslaved people in the south are declared free on 1 January in President Abraham Lincoln's Emancipation Proclamation. This marks a turning point for the war, as Lincoln confirms that the war is a war for freedom, thus strengthening the Union's resolve.

1863

Slavery abolished

The Emancipation Proclamation frees enslaved people, but does not end slavery itself. The 13th Amendment to the US Constitution brings a permanent end to slavery in all of the United States, including new territories. It remains legal, however, as a punishment for crime. Since 1619, tens of millions of enslaved people had died as a result of slavery.

1865

Slave triangle

At least ten million Africans were taken to the Americas in a triangle of trade. Ships from Britain carried manufactured goods such as cloth, ironware, and guns to West Africa. These were exchanged for enslaved men, women, and children. The conditions on the sea crossing to the West Indies were brutal, and many enslaved people did not survive them. Those who did were sold at auctions, and the profits were used to buy sugar, cotton, rum, and tobacco to take back to Britain.

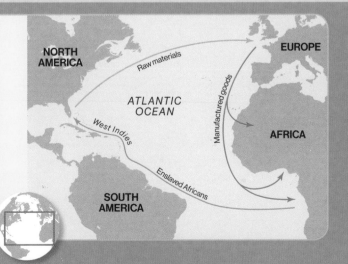

NORTH AMERICA

Raw materials

EUROPE

ATLANTIC OCEAN

Manufactured goods

West Indies

AFRICA

Enslaved Africans

SOUTH AMERICA

Seeking equality
Formerly enslaved people speak out about inequality. When local plantation owners fail to grant citizenship to wealthy formerly enslaved people, fighting breaks out.

1790

Tensions rise
Simmering tensions lead to a slave rebellion in Saint-Domingue. Plantation houses are set on fire and enslavers are killed. Toussaint helps his former enslaver and wife escape. He secures his own family's safety, before joining the rebellion.

1791

Joining forces
As fighting between the rebels and the plantation owners continues, Toussaint joins the rebels under the leader of the revolt, Georges Biassou. Toussaint becomes his military commander.

1791

War
War breaks out between French colony Saint-Domingue and Spanish colony Santo Domingo, both fighting to control the island. Britain fears the rebellion will spread to its colony, Jamaica, and sends troops to end the revolt.

1793

Becoming L'Ouverture
Commanders of the rebellion join the Spanish to fight against the French. Toussaint successfully leads a 4,000-troop army. He adopts the surname L'Ouverture (meaning "the one who opened the way"), from the French word for "opening".

1793

Marriage
Toussaint marries Suzanne Simone Baptiste, his godfather's daughter. He adopts Suzanne's son, Placide, and they have two sons together, Isaac and Saint-Jean.

1782...

Free
At the age of 33, Toussaint is freed. Toussaint's former enslaver, land owner's son, buys land on the plantation and owns it himself. He rents land to enslaved people, who he later frees. Toussaint continues to work for his former enslaver's family.

1776...

Educated
He grows up on a slave plantation. Toussaint's godfather, a freed enslaved person, teaches him to read and write. He learns some French, as well as Creole.

1763...

Born into slavery
Toussaint is born into an enslaved family in Saint-Domingue, on the Caribbean island of Hispaniola. According to a family story, he is the grandson of a prince from the West African kingdom of Arada.

c.1743

Jean-Jacques Dessalines (1758–1806)
Like Toussaint L'Ouverture, Jean-Jacques Dessalines was born into enslavement in Saint-Domingue. He joined the slave rebellion in 1791, and rose through the army ranks to lead many successful campaigns. In 1803, Dessalines defeated the last of Napoleon's forces, and proclaimed independence for Haiti on 1 January 1804, making the country the first Black independent republic. Dessalines became the country's first ruler.

Toussaint L'Ouverture

Born into enslavement in the French colony of Saint-Domingue (modern-day Haiti), Toussaint L'Ouverture (c.1743–1803) led a successful slave rebellion against colonial rule. His actions paved the way to establishing Haiti as an independent Black-governed state, and inspired others in the Americas to resist colonial rule.

Switching sides

With its rule over Saint-Domingue threatened, the French abolish enslavement across their empire. Spain and Britain refuse to do the same, leading Toussaint to change his allegiance to France. He inspires his troops to follow him.

1794

Leading the way

Toussaint forces the French to declare him Lieutenant Governor of Saint-Domingue. He expels the British and gains territory from Spain. He introduces a constitution, guaranteeing rights for Black people.

1796...

War with Napoleon

When French ruler Napoleon Bonaparte announces his plan to restore direct rule to the island, Toussaint prepares his troops for war. Napoleon dispatches his brother-in-law with troops to Saint-Domingue.

1802

Death

After much fierce fighting against French forces, Toussaint signs a peace treaty. However, he is seized by the French and sent to prison, where he is tortured and dies. In 1804, Saint-Domingue proclaims independence from France.

1803

French colonialism

France began to colonize North America in the 16th century, taking control of much of modern-day Canada, the midwestern United States, and the Caribbean. The colony of Saint-Domingue, on the Caribbean island of Hispaniola, was established in 1659. Its slave plantations provided sugar and coffee to France. In the 18th century, slave rebellions and conflicts with colonial rivals led to France losing most of its colonies in North America and the Caribbean.

TOUSSAINT L'OUVERTURE'S SWORD

Olaudah Equiano

Kidnapped and enslaved as a child from the Kingdom of Benin (modern-day Nigeria), Olaudah Equiano (1745–1797) dedicated his life to abolishing slavery. After settling in Britain, he wrote about his experiences as an enslaved person in his autobiography, which went on to have a powerful impact on public opinion. Equiano did not live to see the abolition of the slave trade, but his story deeply influenced the abolitionist cause, and encouraged other formerly enslaved people to tell their stories, too.

Ownership
In the British colony of Virginia, Olaudah is sold to Michael Pascal, an officer in the British Royal Navy. It is common practice for owners of enslaved people to rename their captives, as a way of further stripping their identity away. Pascal renames Olaudah "Gustavus Vassa".

Life at sea
Olaudah spends several years at sea as Pascal's valet (personal servant) during the Seven Years' War between Britain and France. He becomes an experienced seafarer, and carries gunpowder onto ships' decks during battles.

Cheated
While enslaved to Pascal, Olaudah is baptized as a Christian and later learns to read and write. Having fought for the British, Olaudah is led to believe that he should gain his freedom, but Pascal cheats him and Olaudah remains enslaved.

Enslaved
Olaudah is born in the Igbo region of modern-day Nigeria – then part of the Kingdom of Benin. At the age of 11, he and his sister are kidnapped, enslaved, and taken across the Atlantic Ocean to the Americas.

1745...

1756

1758...

1759...

Slave ship
This model shows the appallingly cramped conditions inside the *Brookes*, a British slave ship. The model was widely reproduced to raise awareness of the evils of the slave trade.

Slavery stories

Olaudah Equiano's writing became the blueprint for other enslaved people to write about their own experiences. These narratives helped contribute to the movement to abolish slavery.

Jupiter Hammon (c.1711–1806)

Like Olaudah, Hammon had been enslaved, and used his experiences to argue for abolition. In 1760, he became the first African American to have a poem – called "An Evening Thought" – published. He is regarded as a founder of African American literature.

Phillis Wheatley (c.1753–1784)

Phillis Wheatley was transported from Africa to Boston in British America, where she was sold to a merchant who taught her to read and write. She became a poet, and was the first African American woman to have her work published.

Harriet Jacobs (1813–1897)

After escaping slavery in 1842, Harriet Jacobs documented her experiences in her autobiography, *Incidents in the Life of a Slave Girl*. She became involved with the abolitionists associated with the *North Star* newspaper, set up by prominent African American abolitionist Frederick Douglass.

Freedom

Olaudah works as a deckhand and valet for King, and earns money as a trader, selling sugar and fruit. After three years, he has earned enough to pay King the exact sum of money he was bought for. By the age of 21 he is free.

Zong massacre

The captain of a British slave ship, the *Zong*, throws 133 enslaved people overboard in the mid-Atlantic so that the ship owner can claim insurance for what is considered the loss of "human cargo". The barbarism of this act helps Olaudah and other abolitionists to alert the public to the cruelty of the slave trade.

Sons of Africa

In London, Olaudah joins with 11 other leaders of the Black community to form the Sons of Africa, a group that campaigns for slavery to be abolished.

Sold

Olaudah is sold twice, and ends up enslaved to Robert King, a wealthy merchant, on the Caribbean island of Montserrat. Witnessing the torture of other enslaved Africans reignites Olaudah's desire to gain his freedom as soon as possible.

Exploring the world

Olaudah uses the skills he has learned as a sailor to explore and discover the world. One voyage, led by English explorer Constantine Phipps, takes him to the Arctic on a mission to find out if the seas there are navigable.

Settling in Britain

On his voyages, Olaudah runs the risk of being re-enslaved. He decides to settle in London, England, where his right to be free is most likely to be protected, even though slavery is still legal there.

Leading voice

By now, Olaudah is the leading voice on African issues in London, and his comments on topics such as slavery are reported in the newspapers.

1762   1766...   1773...   1781   1784   1786   1788   1789   1797

Autobiography

Olaudah describes the horrors of slavery in his book *The Interesting Narrative of the Life of Olaudah Equiano, or Gustavus Vassa, the African*. It is a huge success, and profoundly influences public opinion. Olaudah spends many months publicly speaking about his life and enslavement.

Death

Olaudah dies at the age of 52. His work and the work of other abolitionists, results in the slave trade being made illegal in the British Empire in 1807. Slavery itself was abolished completely in most British colonies in 1833.

Mary Seacole

Jamaican-born nurse Mary Seacole (1805–1881) dedicated her life to caring for the sick. After her offer to help save lives as a nurse during the Crimean War (1853–1856) in eastern Europe was rejected by the British government, she funded her own trip to the battlefields. There she became known as "Mother Seacole" by the grateful soldiers she cared for. After her death, her remarkable achievements were forgotten for more than a century, but now she is once again recognized as a hero.

> **"The grateful words... which rewarded me for binding up a wound... was a pleasure worth risking life for".**
>
> **Mary Seacole,**
> ***Wonderful Adventures of Mrs Seacole in Many Lands* (1857)**

Pioneering health workers

At a time of great improvement in nursing standards, these African American nurses helped to save countless lives with their dedication to their profession.

Mary Eliza Mahoney (1845–1926)
Born to formerly enslaved parents, Mary Eliza Mahoney was one of the first African American women to become a registered nurse. She established an organization to help promote African Americans in the nursing profession. She fought for women's equality and for women to be able to vote.

Susie Taylor (1848–1912)
Susie Taylor was the first African American Army nurse. She tended to soldiers fighting in the US Civil War. She was never paid for her work. After the war, she became the first African American to open and teach at a school for formerly enslaved African Americans.

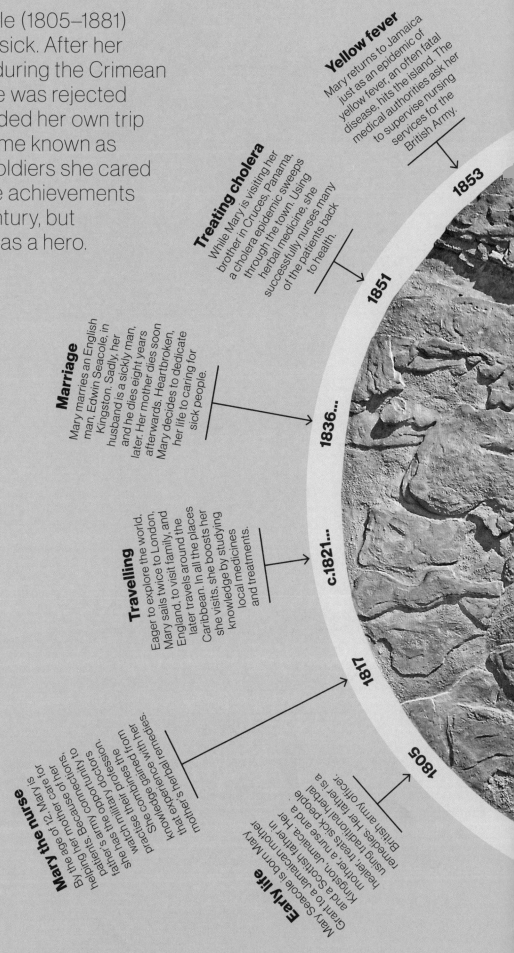

Yellow fever
Mary returns to Jamaica just as an epidemic of yellow fever, an often fatal disease, hits the island. The medical authorities ask her to supervise nursing services for the British Army.

1853

Treating cholera
While Mary is visiting her brother in Cruces, Panama, a cholera epidemic sweeps through the town. Using herbal medicine, she successfully nurses many of the patients back to health.

1851

Marriage
Mary marries an English man, Edwin Seacole, in Kingston. Sadly, her husband is a sickly man, and he dies eight years later. Her mother dies soon afterwards. Heartbroken, Mary decides to dedicate her life to caring for sick people.

1836...

Travelling
Eager to explore the world, Mary sails twice to London, England, to visit family, and later travels around the Caribbean. In all the places she visits, she boosts her knowledge by studying local medicines and treatments.

c.1821...

Mary the nurse
By the age of 12, Mary is caring for her mother care for her patients. Because connections to helping her mother's army doctors father's army profession she has military profession practise combined with her knowledge gained with her. She experience combined from that experience gained from mother's herbal remedies.

1817

Early life
Mary Seacole is born Mary Grant to a Jamaican mother and a Scottish father in Kingston, Jamaica. Her mother, a nurse and a healer, treats sick people using traditional herbal remedies. Her father is a British army officer.

1805

Crimean War

The Crimean War, a conflict in eastern Europe between Britain and its allies and the Russian Empire, breaks out. When Mary hears about the British military's poor medical facilities, she travels to England and asks to be sent to the area as an army nurse. Refused by the British government, she decides to fund her own trip.

British Hotel

In the Crimea, Mary and her friend Thomas Day build the British Hotel, a makeshift restaurant and shop where soldiers can rest, and buy food and medical supplies. She treats the wounded, and delivers rations to the front line. The troops call her "Mother Seacole".

Back to England

Mary returns to England with little money, and declares herself bankrupt. She survives at first on donations from the public.

1853

1855

July 1856

Telling her story

Mary's autobiography, The Wonderful Adventures of Mrs Seacole in Many Lands, is published. In it, she gives her account of caring for the sick and coping with the constant barrage of missiles during the war.

July 1857

Royal connections

As Mary's celebrity grows, she becomes known in royal circles. A nephew of Queen Victoria carves a statue of her, which is later exhibited at the Royal Academy. She becomes a nurse to Alexandra of Denmark, the Princess of Wales and wife of the future King Edward VII.

1871...

Death

Mary spends her last years living quietly. She dies in her home in London.

1881

STATUE OF MARY SEACOLE BY SCULPTOR MARTIN JENNINGS OUTSIDE ST THOMAS' HOSPITAL IN LONDON

WONDERFUL ADVENTURES of Mrs SEACOLE

LONDON JAMES BLACKWOOD

1845

"You have seen how a man was made a slave; you shall see how a slave was made a man".

Narrative of the Life of Frederick Douglass, An American Slave (1845)

Having delivered his first anti-slavery speech in 1841, Douglass is now an established public speaker. He writes the first of three volumes of his autobiography. It's a huge success, but Douglass worries that his old enslaver will find him because of his growing fame and claim him back. He decides to leave the US, and travels around Ireland and the UK. Two years later, two Englishmen 'purchase' his freedom by paying off his former enslaver.

1838

"I prayed for freedom for twenty years, but received no answer until I prayed with my legs".

Narrative of the Life of Frederick Douglass, An American Slave (1845)

Two years after a failed attempt, Frederick successfully escapes by hopping on a train heading north, to the anti-slavery states. He is helped by his fiancée, a free African American woman named Anna Murray, and they marry. He changes his surname to Douglass to divert attention from himself. He becomes a preacher, and begins to campaign against slavery.

1826

"I set out... at whatever cost of trouble, to learn how to read".

Narrative of the Life of Frederick Douglass, An American Slave (1845)

Aged eight, Frederick is sent to work for a new white enslaver in Baltimore. The enslaver's wife teaches him to read, but her husband stops the lessons, worried that reading will lead Frederick to demand his freedom. The boy,

1847

"Right is of no sex – Truth is of no colour".

Slogan of The North Star newspaper

Returning to the US, Douglass sets up a weekly anti-slavery newspaper, *The North Star*, in New York. The paper advocates women's rights, as well as the abolition of slavery.

1861

"Let the slaves be... formed into a liberating army, to march into the South and raise the banner of Emancipation".

"How To End the War", Douglass' Monthly (1861)

The Civil War breaks out in the US, with slavery as a central point of difference between the anti-slavery Union in the north and pro-slavery Confederacy in the south. Douglass argues that African Americans should be allowed to fight for their freedom for the Union.

1864

"[Lincoln] did not let me feel for a moment that there was any difference in the color of our skins".

About Abraham Lincoln (1864)

President Abraham Lincoln's Emancipation Proclamation declares the freedom of all enslaved people in Confederate-held territory. Douglass is critical of Lincoln's late conversion to abolition but recognizes his hatred of slavery, and the two become friendly.

Frederick Douglass

A formerly enslaved person, African American Frederick Douglass (c.1818–1895) was the leading campaigner against slavery of his time. He was a brilliant public speaker and wrote a best-selling autobiography, which powerfully described the effect of slavery on the enslaved. In his later years, he acted as an advisor to President Abraham Lincoln during the US Civil War, and campaigned for equal rights for all people right up to the end of his life.

c.1818

"I do not recollect ever seeing my mother by the light of day... She would lie down with me, and get me to sleep, but long before I **waked she was gone**".

Narrative of the Life of Frederick Douglass, An American Slave (1845)

Frederick Bailey is born into slavery in Maryland, the son of an enslaved woman and an unknown white man. He is separated from his mother as an infant, and lives with her parents.

1867

"Let no man be kept from **the ballot box because of his colour**".

From a speech (1867)

The passage of the Thirteenth Amendment to the US Constitution brings slavery in the US to an end forever. Douglass switches his attention to African American rights. He supports Ulysses S. Grant as president in the 1868 election. Grant wins, and he supports guaranteeing African Americans the right to vote, which is granted in 1870 in the Fifteenth Amendment.

1883...

"No man can put a chain about the ankle of his fellow man without at last finding the other end fastened about his own neck".

From a speech at Civil Rights Mass Meeting, Washington, D.C. (1883)

Douglass continues giving powerful speeches well into old age, lecturing and writing in support of civil rights. He dies in 1895 after giving a speech to the National Council of Women.

Harriet Tubman

In the southern states of the US, Harriet Tubman (c.1822–1913) battled enslavement and disability to help more than 70 enslaved people escape captivity. She achieved this through a secret network known as the Underground Railroad. In later years, she became a passionate speaker for women's right to vote.

Harsh conditions

Harriet is born Araminta ("Minty") Ross in Maryland, US, into an enslaved family. She endures cruel beatings by enslavers as a child. Aged around 12, she is hit on the head with a heavy metal weight. The injury causes her lifelong seizures and hallucinations.

1822...

Harpers Ferry

Harriet's success gains her respect among other abolitionists (people looking to end slavery). She helps leading abolitionist John Brown recruit for a planned raid on a US arsenal at Harpers Ferry, Virginia, which he hopes will start a slave revolt. However, the raid fails and Brown is executed.

Civil war

Civil war breaks out between the slave-owning Confederate states of the south and the anti-slavery Union states of the north. Harriet welcomes the war as an opportunity to advance the abolitionist cause. She works as a nurse, but is soon helping recruit African American soldiers to fight for the Union.

Moses

Harriet mounts 13 successful missions in total. She uses her growing network of trusted friends and contacts to rescue many family members, as well as 50-60 additional people. She earns the nickname "Moses", after the biblical prophet who led the Hebrews to safety.

1861... **1859** **1851**

Female activists of the 19th century

Before the 19th century, women's opinions on how society should work were rarely taken into account. As the abolition cause grew, Black female activists began to speak out about slavery and women's issues.

Sojourner Truth (1797–1883)

African American activist Sojourner Truth was born Isabella Baumfree to enslaved parents. After escaping and gaining freedom in 1826, she campaigned passionately for abolition and women's rights, delivering heartfelt speeches across the nation. Truth would often point to her own muscles, gained during her years of slave labour, to demonstrate a woman's strength.

Maria W. Stewart (1803–1879)

After losing both her parents at the age of five, Maria W. Stewart went on to become a teacher, journalist, and activist. In the 1830s, she became the first African American to lecture for the causes of abolition and women's rights.

Combahee River Raid

Harriet leads a group of armed scouts through South Carolina's swamps and marshes, providing key army intelligence. She becomes the first woman in charge of an armed assault during the Civil War when she guides Union steamboats along the Combahee River safely past the Confederate fire. Once ashore, Union troops set several plantations ablaze, liberating more than 700 enslaved people.

Humanitarian work

The Union Army wins the Civil War, and slavery is finally abolished across the US. Harriet starts a new career helping formerly enslaved people and the poor, but struggles for money, having been denied compensation for her role in the war.

1863 **1865...**

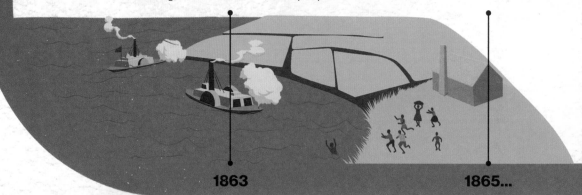

Dreams of freedom

She marries a free Black man, John Tubman, and around this time she decides to name herself "Harriet", which was her mother's name. She sets her heart on escaping slavery by fleeing to the north (where slavery is illegal), but her husband does not share her dream.

1844

Underground Railroad

When Harriet's enslaver dies, she fears she will be sold and separated from her family. While "loaned" out to another plantation, she escapes by using a network of trusted people and safe houses known as the Underground Railroad. She reaches the free state of Pennsylvania.

1849

Underground Railroad

The Underground Railroad was not a literal railway. Instead, it was a network of secret routes and safe houses organized by Black and white abolitionists along which fleeing enslaved people (or "passengers") could travel to reach safety in the northern US or Canada. Small bands of runaways, led by a guide or "conductor", kept well away from towns, crossing forests, swamps, and mountain trails to escape detection by slave catchers. In total, the Underground Railroad is estimated to have taken about 100,000 enslaved people to freedom.

Growing confidence

After successfully rescuing her brother, Harriet returns to Maryland to find her husband, only to discover he has married another woman. Instead, she leads a group of 11 people safely to Canada, her most daring mission yet.

1851

First rescue

Congress passes the Fugitive Slave Act, which punishes those helping enslaved people to escape. Despite the risks, Harriet vows to return to Maryland to rescue her family. Using her knowledge of the swamps and forests, she leads her niece and her niece's two children to safety.

1850

This was the slogan of the National Association of Coloured Women, which fought for women's rights.

LIFTING AS WE CLIMB

Home for the aged

Harriet donates land to open a home for elderly and poverty-stricken African Americans. She dies there of pneumonia in 1913, surrounded by friends and family.

Women's rights

Harriet becomes actively involved in the movement to give women the vote. She is finally granted an army pension in 1899.

Biting the bullet

Harriet undergoes brain surgery in an attempt to treat the head trauma she has suffered since childhood. She refuses an anaesthetic, choosing instead to bite on a bullet, as Civil War soldiers had during their operations.

1890s...

1898

1903–1913

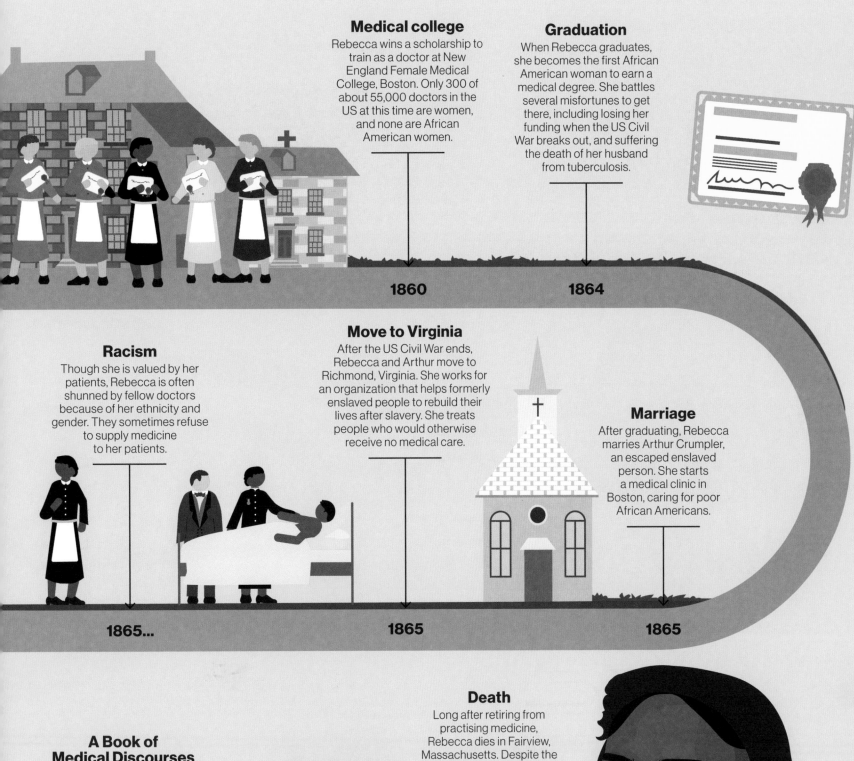

Medical college

Rebecca wins a scholarship to train as a doctor at New England Female Medical College, Boston. Only 300 of about 55,000 doctors in the US at this time are women, and none are African American women.

1860

Graduation

When Rebecca graduates, she becomes the first African American woman to earn a medical degree. She battles several misfortunes to get there, including losing her funding when the US Civil War breaks out, and suffering the death of her husband from tuberculosis.

1864

Racism

Though she is valued by her patients, Rebecca is often shunned by fellow doctors because of her ethnicity and gender. They sometimes refuse to supply medicine to her patients.

1865...

Move to Virginia

After the US Civil War ends, Rebecca and Arthur move to Richmond, Virginia. She works for an organization that helps formerly enslaved people to rebuild their lives after slavery. She treats people who would otherwise receive no medical care.

1865

Marriage

After graduating, Rebecca marries Arthur Crumpler, an escaped enslaved person. She starts a medical clinic in Boston, caring for poor African Americans.

1865

A Book of Medical Discourses

Now living in Hyde Park, New York, Rebecca turns the journal notes she has kept during her years of medical practice into a book. *A Book of Medical Discourses* gives advice to women on how to care for themselves and their children.

1883

Death

Long after retiring from practising medicine, Rebecca dies in Fairview, Massachusetts. Despite the many obstacles placed in her way, she has achieved much in her career, and is an inspiration to many who came after her.

There are no confirmed portraits of Rebecca. This one is based on how medical workers of her time dressed.

1895

Family changes

When Lewis is 10 years old, his father leaves his mother and their four children. Some years after, Lewis finishes school and goes to work as an office assistant for a prominent lawyer.

Return to Boston

After a year of serving in the Navy – and with the Union emerging victorious – Lewis is given an honourable discharge, meaning he is allowed to return home. He returns to Boston to find work.

Drafting

At the firm, Lewis teaches himself the skill of drafting – the job of creating detailed technical drawings of inventions for patent applications. Upon seeing his drafting excellence, his law firm promotes him to the position of draftsman, then chief draftsman.

Born in Boston

Lewis is born in Boston, Massachusetts, US. His parents, George and Rebecca, are formerly enslaved people who escaped their enslavers in Virginia. Lewis is the youngest of their four children.

Civil War

When Lewis is 12, civil war breaks out between the northern and southern states of the US. When he reaches the age of 16, he enlists in the Navy, to fight for the Union (northern) forces.

Law firm

Lewis finds work as an office assistant at Crosby, Halstead & Gould, a Boston-based law firm specializing in patents. Patents are special licenses that protect the work of inventors from being copied or stolen.

Family life

Lewis meets and falls in love with Mary Wilson. The couple marry in December 1873 in Fall River, Massachusetts. They go on to have two daughters, Emma Jeanette and Louise Rebecca.

1848 **1858...** **1861...** **1865** **1865** **1866...** **1873...**

1928 **1925**

Ignored inventors

The work of Black inventors has often been ignored or forgotten. However, the modern world would be very different without the many innovations and contributions that Black inventors have given us.

Sarah Boone (1832–1904)

African American inventor Sarah Boone patented and developed the ironing board in 1892. Her invention improved the quality of ironing, and is the origin of the product we still use today.

Garrett Morgan (1877–1963)

Before African American inventor Garrett Morgan, traffic lights only signalled for "Stop" and "Go". He developed the three-position system we still use today. He also created an early version of the gas mask.

Marie Van Brittan Brown (1922–1999)

Feeling unsafe if she was ever home alone at night, African American Marie Van Brittan Brown created a home security system. It used a camera and peepholes, and allowed for safe recognition of visitors who came to her door.

Death and legacy

Lewis dies at the age of 80. Sixty years later, his whole home is moved to Flushing, New York, where it serves as a museum to celebrate science, and to remember his many contributions to his eventful life.

Published poet

Lewis' career gradually comes to a close as his eyesight begins to fail, meaning he can't continue to work on patent drawings. He finds other interests, including painting, playwriting, playing the flute, and writing poetry. A collection of his work, titled Poems of Love and Life, is published.

Lewis Howard Latimer

An inventor, engineer, and writer, Lewis Howard Latimer was a key figure in the development of some of the most revolutionary inventions of the 19th century. Though the importance of his work is often overlooked, his contributions have changed the way people live today.

Telephone

After inventing the first working telephone, Scottish-born inventor Alexander Graham Bell asks Lewis to assist him on the patent application for his invention. Lewis creates the drawings required to receive the patent for it.

New job

Lewis and his family move to Connecticut, where he meets American-born inventor Hiram Maxim. Impressed by his drafting skills, Hiram offers Lewis a draftsman job at his Electric Lighting Company.

Carbon filament

While working at the Electric Lighting Company, Lewis sees a way of improving American inventor (and Maxim's rival) Thomas Edison's light bulb. Lewis invents and patents the carbon filament, which allows the bulb to last longer than it did with the paper filament that Edison's design used.

Working for Edison

Following the success of his carbon filament, Lewis is hired by Edison's Electric Light Company. He is employed as a draftsman and an expert on the patents of electric lights. He later becomes chief draftsman at the company.

Author

Lewis writes the first book on electric lighting, *Incandescent Electric Lighting*. On top of his daily work, he teaches technical drawing to immigrants and helps establish the Unitarian church in Flushing, New York.

Edison Pioneers

At the age of 70, Lewis becomes a member of the Edison Pioneers, a highly prestigious and selective group composed of employees of Thomas Edison. He is the first and only African American to join the organization.

1876
1880
1881
1883...
1890
1918

African Americans and the US Civil War

From 1861 to 1865, the US Civil War raged between northern and southern states over the question of slavery. Despite reluctance on both sides to call African American soldiers up, more than 200,000 eventually fought in the war. They hoped to gain their freedom, but almost a fifth of them died in the fighting, never to return home.

Antietam
The bloodiest single day of the war sees some 23,000 soldiers dead, wounded, or missing after the Battle of Antietam. The battle ends in a Union victory.

New law
The Union desperately needs more soldiers. African Americans have not been allowed to fight for the US Army, but Lincoln passes a new law, allowing enslaved people in southern states to work to support the Union's cause.

Confederate states
To protect their economies – which are based on slave labour – seven southern states leave the United States to create their own Confederate government, with Jefferson Davis as president. The Confederates see themselves as a separate nation. A month later, Abraham Lincoln becomes US president. He sets out to end what he saw as a rebellion.

First Battle of Bull Run
The Union is defeated in the First Battle of Bull Run (also known as the Battle of Manassas) in Virginia. In August 1862, the Confederates win the Second Battle of Bull Run. The Union is so afraid of defeat that it prepares its capital, Washington, D.C., for attack.

September 1862

January 1863

July 1862

February 1861...

April 1861

July 1861...

Emancipation Proclamation
Lincoln introduces the Emancipation Proclamation, an order to free all of the 3.5 million enslaved people in the Confederate states (though the Confederate states still considered them enslaved). It also states that African American soldiers can fight in the Union Army. This declaration marks a change in the Union's reasons for fighting the war, from ending the rebellion to achieving the abolition of slavery.

The war begins
Lincoln refuses to agree to the Confederates' demands to hand over power and property to them. Confederate forces attack Fort Sumter in South Carolina, and the Civil War begins. Four more states leave the United States (known as the Union during the Civil War) to join the Confederate states.

Napoleon Field Gun
Named after the French emperor Napoleon III, this type of cannon was widely used in the Civil War. It could hit a target up to 1,600 m (5,250 ft) away and fire a cannonball at 439 m (1,440 ft) per second.

Fort Wagner assault
The 54th Massachusetts, a regiment of African American soldiers, leads an attack on the Confederate base Fort Wagner. Though the assault is unsuccessful, the bravery and skill of the African American soldiers impresses the Union military leaders. The assault leads to even more African Americans enlisting in the Army.

Thirteenth Amendment
The Thirteenth Amendment to the US Constitution is passed, which abolishes slavery across the US, except as a punishment for crime. Though millions of African Americans were freed during the war, their personal liberty in the US is far from a settled issue.

African American troops
Lincoln's proclamation changes the Union Army. Huge numbers of African Americans, seeking to take part in a conflict that directly affects their lives, offer to fight. The Union creates the Bureau of Colored Troops to organize the coordination of new African American regiments ("colored" is a term for African Americans that is now outdated and offensive).

Surrender meeting
After an attempt to break through Union lines fails, Confederate commander Robert E. Lee realizes that the Confederates cannot win the war. He meets Union general Ulysses S. Grant at Appomattox Court House, Virginia, to surrender. Though the war is essentially over, some fighting continues.

July 1863　　**November 1863**　　**April 1865**　　**April 1865**　　**May 1865...**　　**December 1865...**

May 1863　　**July 1863**

Gettysburg Address
President Lincoln delivers his most famous speech at the dedication of the Soldiers' National Cemetery in Gettysburg. He declares the Civil War to be a struggle for freedom and equality for all Americans, including African Americans.

Lincoln assassinated
At a play in Washington, D.C., President Lincoln is shot by John Wilkes Booth, an actor hoping to avenge the Confederates. Lincoln dies the next morning.

Gettysburg
The Battle of Gettysburg in Pennsylvania proves to be a turning point of the war. The Union emerges victorious, and finally ends Confederate hopes of invading the Union states. It is the bloodiest multi-day conflict in the history of the Civil War.

War is over
The rest of the Confederate armies give up the fight. Both sides agree surrender terms, including the ending of slavery. New president Andrew Johnson declares the official end of the Civil War. On 19 June, the last group of enslaved African Americans is told of their liberation – a date celebrated every year since as "Juneteenth".

African Americans during the war
African Americans performed a number of roles in both the Union and Confederate forces during the Civil War. In the Confederate Army, African American men were not allowed to fight or carry weapons – they worked only as labourers. After the Emancipation Proclamation, African American soldiers fought alongside white soldiers in the Union Army, and also had their own regiments, but were paid 30 per cent less (they received equal pay after June 1864). African American seamen in the Union Navy were paid the same as their white counterparts. Though forbidden from signing up officially, many African American women contributed to the Union's cause, working as nurses, scouts, and spies.

A REGIMENT OF AFRICAN AMERICAN SOLDIERS

The 54th Massachusetts

This detail is from the memorial to the 54th Massachusetts Infantry Regiment in Boston, US. Formed in February 1863, the 54th Massachusetts was one of the first major American military units of African American soldiers to fight in the US Civil War.
Its troops took part in many operations, including the attack on Fort Wagner. Roughly 178,000 Black soldiers served in approximately 175 regiments during the war, making up about 10 per cent of the Union Army's soldiers. Their skills, heroism, and determination were decisive factors in the Union's eventual victory.

Early years
Hoping to build a happier and more stable life for herself, Sarah gets married. Sarah gives birth to a daughter, A'Lelia, in 1885. Tragedy strikes again, however, when her husband dies in 1887, leaving Sarah alone with the child to care for.

Childhood
Sarah Breedlove is born in Louisiana, US. She is the child of recently freed enslaved people Minerva and Owen Breedlove. By the time she is seven, Sarah has become an orphan, and lives with her sister Louvinia.

Business idea
After moving north to St. Louis, Sarah works cleaning laundry. She begins losing her hair due to stress and other factors, but there are few hair products available for African American people. Sarah starts to experiment with making her own hair products, and sells them to her neighbours.

Developing an image
Sarah moves to Denver, and a year later, marries Charles J. Walker. Her husband has experience in advertising, and helps Sarah to promote her business. Sarah sells her products under the name "Madam C. J. Walker". They begin to sell in greater numbers.

A growing business
Sarah travels across the southern states of the US to market her products to new customers. She speaks to people in their homes, and even shows them how to use her products at schools and churches.

Empowering women
Sarah opens a beauty college and factory in Pittsburgh, Pennsylvania. The college teaches African American women how to make and sell their own beauty products. This allows them to become more financially independent.

1867...

1882...

c.1904...

1905...

1907

1908

> "There is no royal flower-strewn road to success... what success I have obtained is the result of many sleepless nights and real hard work".
>
> **Sarah Breedlove, *in a speech made to her employees* (1917)**

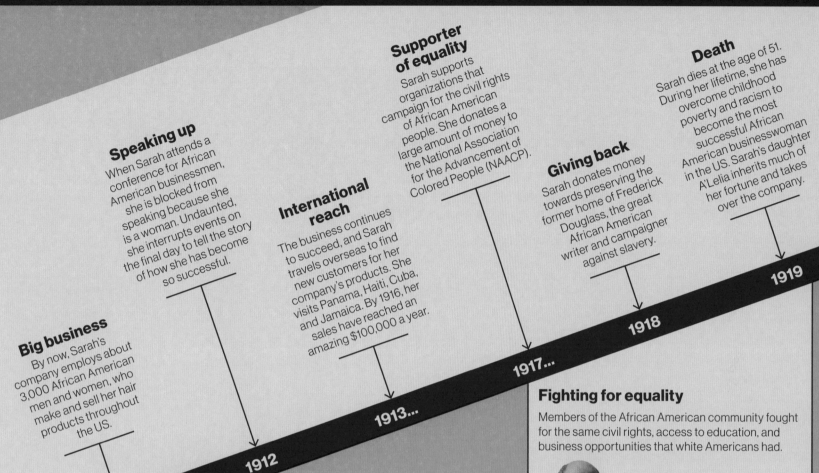

Speaking up
When Sarah attends a conference for African American businessmen, she is blocked from speaking because she is a woman. Undaunted, she interrupts events on the final day to tell the story of how she has become so successful.

Supporter of equality
Sarah supports organizations that campaign for the civil rights of African American people. She donates a large amount of money to the National Association for the Advancement of Colored People (NAACP).

Death
Sarah dies at the age of 51. During her lifetime, she has overcome childhood poverty and racism to become the most successful African American businesswoman in the US. Sarah's daughter A'Lelia inherits much of her fortune and takes over the company.

International reach
The business continues to succeed, and Sarah travels overseas to find new customers for her company's products. She visits Panama, Haiti, Cuba, and Jamaica. By 1916, her sales have reached an amazing $100,000 a year.

Giving back
Sarah donates money towards preserving the former home of Frederick Douglass, the great African American writer and campaigner against slavery.

Big business
By now, Sarah's company employs about 3,000 African American men and women, who make and sell her hair products throughout the US.

1910 **1912** **1913...** **1917...** **1918** **1919**

Sarah Breedlove

At a time when most African Americans faced discrimination and limited business opportunities, inventor and businessperson Sarah Breedlove (1867–1919) became rich developing and selling beauty products. She later shared much of her wealth, donating it to causes that empowered the African American community.

Fighting for equality

Members of the African American community fought for the same civil rights, access to education, and business opportunities that white Americans had.

W. E. B. Du Bois (1868–1963)
Author and activist W. E. B. Du Bois was one of the most important leaders in the fight for full civil rights for African Americans. He helped set up the NAACP, which remains the most important African American civil rights organization.

Mary McLeod Bethune (1875–1955)
An African American educator and campaigner, Mary McLeod Bethune opened a boarding school for Black girls. In time, it became a college offering degree-level courses. After women in the US won the right to vote in 1920, she strongly encouraged her students to register to vote.

Annie Turnbo Malone (1869–1957)
Businesswoman Annie Turnbo Malone became one of the first African American millionaires. Malone set up the Poro Company, which produced popular hair and beauty products for the African American community. She hired the young Sarah Breedlove as one of her door-to-door sales agents.

Colonialism in Africa

Although the slave trade had ravaged Africa for centuries, European powers controlled just 10 per cent of the continent in 1870. The next 30 years saw European nations compete for control of Africa. By 1900, they had seized 90 per cent of African land. It would take more than half a century for these countries to gain their independence back.

Scramble for Africa

This map shows the domination of European powers in Africa by the end of the 19th century. France and Britain colonized the largest areas of land across the continent. Only Liberia and Ethiopia held onto their independence.

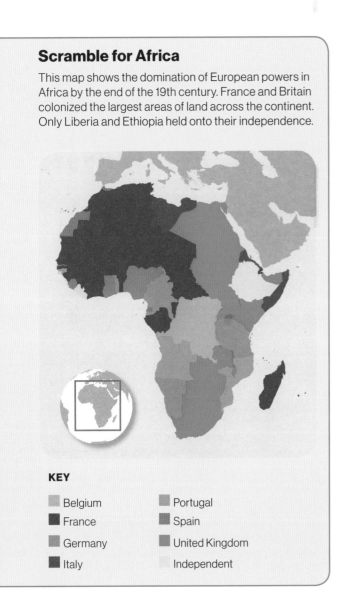

KEY

- Belgium
- France
- Germany
- Italy
- Portugal
- Spain
- United Kingdom
- Independent

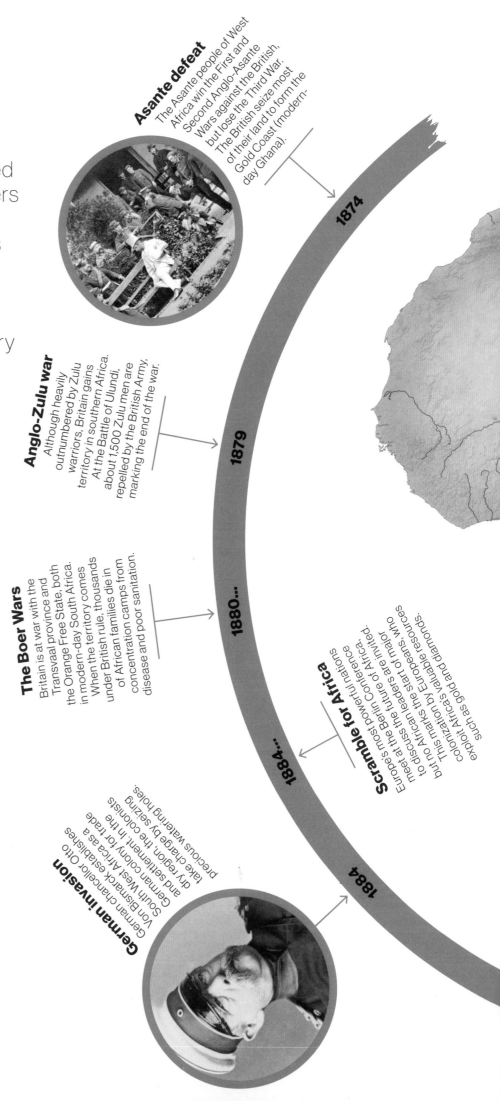

Asante defeat

The Asante people of West Africa win the First and Second Anglo-Asante Wars against the British, but lose the Third War. The British seize most of their land to form the Gold Coast (modern-day Ghana).

1874

Anglo-Zulu war

Although heavily outnumbered by Zulu warriors, Britain gains territory in southern Africa. At the Battle of Ulundi, about 1,500 Zulu men are repelled by the British Army, marking the end of the war.

1879

The Boer Wars

Britain is at war with the Transvaal province and the Orange Free State, both in modern-day South Africa. When the territory comes under British rule, thousands of African families die in concentration camps from disease and poor sanitation.

1880...

Scramble for Africa

Europe's most powerful nations meet at the Berlin Conference. The future of Africa is discussed by major European leaders, who start to divide up African resources. This marks the start of mass colonization by Europeans, but no African is invited. They exploit Africa's gold and diamonds, such as valuable resources.

1884...

German invasion

Von Bismarck establishes South West Africa as a German colony for trade and settlement. In the dry region, the colonists take charge by seizing precious watering holes.

1884

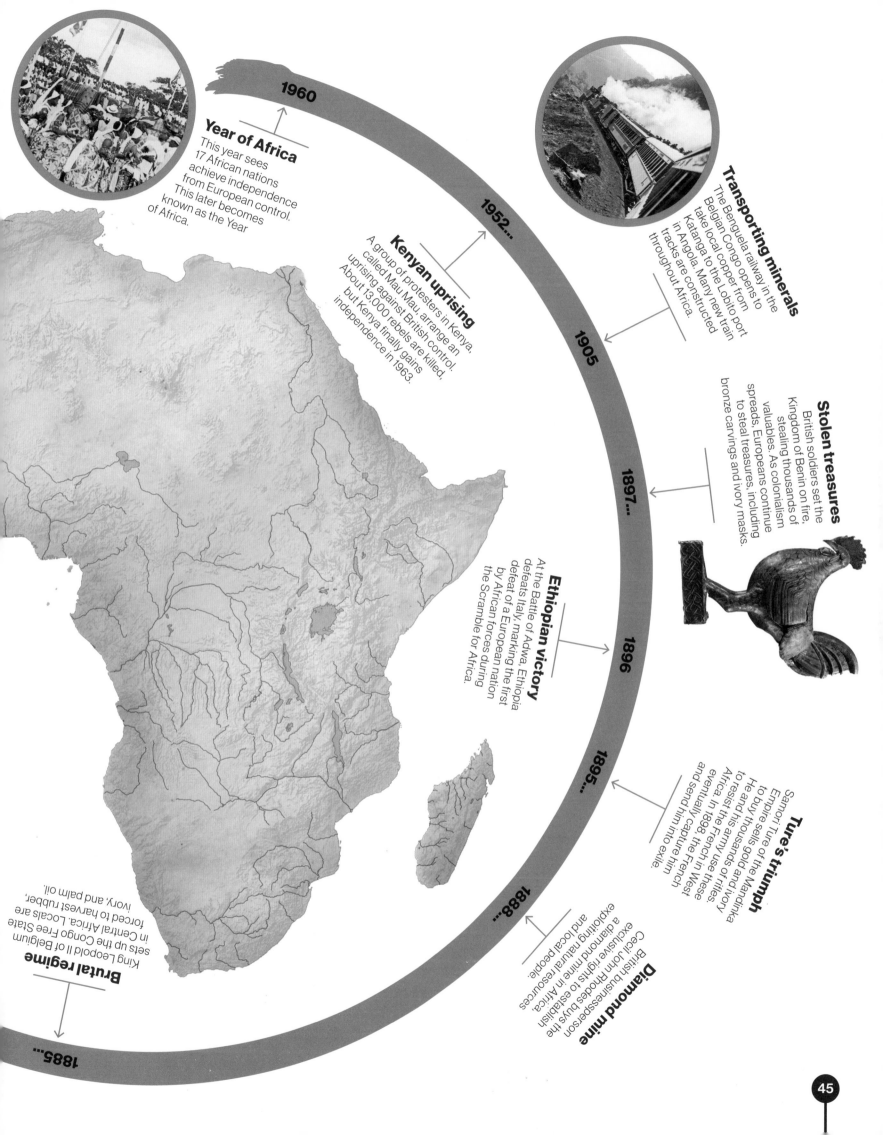

Year of Africa

This year sees 17 African nations achieve independence from European control. This later becomes known as the Year of Africa.

1960

Transporting minerals

The Benguela railway in the Belgian Congo opens to take local copper from Katanga to the Lobito port in Angola. Many new train tracks are constructed throughout Africa.

1952...

Kenyan uprising

A group of protesters in Kenya, called Mau Mau, arrange an uprising against British control. About 13,000 rebels are killed, but Kenya finally gains independence in 1963.

1905

Stolen treasures

British soldiers set the Kingdom of Benin on fire, stealing thousands of valuables. As colonialism spreads, Europeans continue to steal treasures, including bronze carvings and ivory masks.

1897...

Ethiopian victory

At the Battle of Adwa, Ethiopia defeats Italy, marking the first defeat of a European nation by African forces during the Scramble for Africa.

1896

Ture's triumph

Samori Ture of the Wassoulou Empire sells off the Mandinka to buy thousands of rifles. He and his army use these to resist the French in West Africa. In 1898, the French eventually capture him and send him into exile.

1895...

Diamond mine

British businessperson Cecil John Rhodes buys the exclusive rights to establish a diamond mine in Africa, exploiting natural resources and local people.

1888...

Brutal regime

King Leopold II of Belgium sets up the Congo Free State in Central Africa. Locals are forced to harvest rubber, ivory, and palm oil.

1885...

45

Zora Neale Hurston

Zora Neale Hurston (1891–1960) was one of the most significant African American writers of the 20th century. She was a leading figure in the Harlem Renaissance – a flowering of African American culture in the 1920s focused on Harlem, New York City. Hurston travelled widely, documenting the stories and traditions of Black people across the US, the Caribbean, and Central America.

Tragedy strikes

Zora is just 13 when her mother dies. Her father remarries and sends Zora away to boarding school. In time, he stops paying the school fees, and Zora is forced to leave. At the age of 16, she joins a theatre company as a maid, and tours with them across the US.

1891...   1904...   1917

Early life

Zora is born in Notasulga, Alabama, but moves with the rest of her family to Eatonville, Florida, at the age of three.

Bending the truth

At the age of 26, Zora goes back to high school in Baltimore, Maryland. To gain admission, she fakes her age, pretending to be 10 years younger than she is. She keeps to this deception for the rest of her life.

Inspiration and inspired

Zora Neale Hurston's work was partly inspired by her friends who were part of the Harlem Renaissance, and has gone on to inspire artists long after her death.

Alain LeRoy Locke (1886–1954)

The gifted scholar and teacher Alain LeRoy Locke was a major figure in the Harlem Renaissance of the 1920s. He brought together African American writers, musicians, and artists, and encouraged them to look to African culture for inspiration.

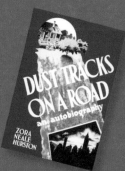

Langston Hughes (1902–1967)

A talented poet, playwright, and novelist, Langston Hughes was a key voice in the Harlem Renaissance. His works celebrated African American culture, spirituality, and humour, and addressed issues such as racism and poverty. Hughes loved the African American musical genre jazz, and often used jazz rhythms in his poetry.

Zadie Smith (b.1975)

English author Zadie Smith's career took off with the publication of her first novel, *White Teeth*, in 2000. The novel is about how Britain treats people who have come from places it once colonized. It was a best-seller and won numerous awards. She has written of her love of Hurston's work, *Their Eyes Were Watching God* in particular.

University studies

Zora continues her studies at Howard University, Washington, D.C. She co-establishes *The Hilltop*, a student newspaper. She also has her first short story, "John Redding Goes to Sea", published in a literary magazine.

Southern travels

Zora travels through the southern US states recording African American folk tales. She meets formerly enslaved person Cudjo Kazoola Lewis, the last survivor of the final slave ship to cross from Africa to the US. She writes a book based on their conversations.

Travels to the Caribbean

Zora is given an award to research the rituals of voodoo (a West African religion) in Haiti, and *obeah* (spiritual healing) in Jamaica. She documents her findings in the book *Tell My Horse*.

Autobiography

Zora's autobiography, *Dust Tracks on a Road*, is published. She gains praise for the quality of her writing. She wins the Anisfield-Wolf Book Award for the book's contribution to the understanding of race relations.

Death

When Zora dies, she is buried in an unmarked grave because there is no money for a headstone. Much later, in 1973, the novelist Alice Walker locates Zora's grave and adds a headstone with the words "Zora Neale Hurston: A Genius of the South".

1921...   **1925...**   **1927...**   **1932...**   **1936...**   **1937**   **1942**   **1950s**   **1960**

Harlem Renaissance

Zora earns a scholarship to study at Barnard College, New York City. She moves to Harlem, a vibrant, mainly African American neighbourhood which is the centre of an explosion of art and ideas called the Harlem Renaissance. She befriends the poet Langston Hughes and other rising stars. They launch a magazine called *Fire!!* in 1926.

Writing

Zora adapts her folk tale research into a play, *The Great Day*, which features folk songs, dance, and pantomime. Two years later, her first novel, *Jonah's Gourd Vine*, is published. Her work is well received, but does not give her mainstream success.

Literary classic

Her second novel, *Their Eyes Were Watching God*, is published. It becomes her most influential book, and many people today see it as a classic of the Harlem Renaissance.

Financial struggles

Zora finds it difficult to get her work published. She takes a job as a substitute teacher in a school, and writes occasional articles for newspapers. She is often underpaid because of her race and gender, and struggles with debt and poverty.

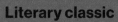

"Mama [told us] to 'jump at de sun'. We might not land on the sun, but at least we would get off the ground".

Zora Neale Hurston,
***Dust Tracks on a Road* (1942)**

TAYTU BETUL

The warrior empress who fought off colonial invasion

As European countries greedily seized huge parts of Africa, Ethiopia was was one of just two African countries that were able to resist. Taytu Betul (1851–1918), the empress of Ethiopia, helped to give her nation the hope and strategy it needed to overcome much better-supplied Italian armies. Her story, and in particular her brave and intelligent leadership during the war with Italy, have been celebrated by Ethiopians ever since.

The Scramble for Africa

For centuries, European countries exploited the natural resources of the African continent. They tended to stay on the coastal areas, though, and rarely ventured inland because they lacked decent maps and reliable ways of getting there. Things began to change in the **19th century**, when technological and medical advances in Europe made it easier to deal with the challenges of the African continent. From **1881**, European countries rushed to seize large parts of the continent for themselves, a period historians call the "Scramble for Africa". In less than 50 years, European countries took 90 per cent of the continent. The European powers rule the African lands they seized as colonies.

Ethiopia and Italy

King Menelik II is the ruler of Shewa, a central region of Ethiopia, a country in East Africa. In **1883**, he marries Taytu Betul. The daughter of an aristocratic family in northern Ethiopia, Taytu is a confident scholar, poet, musician, and chess player. She has strong political ideas, including a desire to resist the spread of European power in Africa. In **1887**, she establishes and names the city of Addis Ababa (meaning "new flower"), which becomes Ethiopia's capital city. Menelik gradually brings more territory under his rule, and is proclaimed emperor of Ethiopia in **1889**. Almost immediately, he signs the Treaty

of Wichale with Italy. In it, the emperor agrees not to attack Italian-ruled territories to the north of Ethiopia (in modern-day Eritrea). However, the Italian version of the treaty gives Italy control over Ethiopia, something that is not in the version in Amharic, Menelik and Taytu's language.

War looms

When the Ethiopians discover the deception, Taytu's worries about European control are confirmed. The relationship between the two countries begins to fall apart. According to some sources, Italy tries to get Menelik and Taytu to accept the treaty. When they refuse, Italy threatens to invade. Knowing that their country's independence is at stake, Menelik and Taytu stand their ground. In **1895**, as war looms, the couple call their people together from across the country. Ethiopians from every tribe, culture, and community gather together to form the army. Though they have inferior weapons to the Italians, their army of 100,000 is larger, and more determined, than Italy expected.

Leading her people

The war begins when Italy invades Ethiopia from the north. The Italians initially make a lot of progress. They get deep into Ethiopian territory before the Ethiopians are able to turn them back. As the war rages, Taytu becomes one of the key people on the

Ethiopian side. Her ability to organize the Ethiopian forces and strategize during battles is a huge asset. She also uses spies to gain information about the Italian forces. During one part of the war, the Italians occupy a secure fort at Mekelle. Taytu gets them to surrender by surrounding the fort and cutting off its water supply – a clever plan that avoids any loss of life on either side.

The Battle of Adwa

The final event of the war takes place at the Battle of Adwa on **1 March 1896**. With supplies running low for both sides, the Italians prepare a surprise attack by marching over the mountain tracks of Adwa. They soon become separated and disorganized. When the Ethiopians realize the Italians are attacking, they quickly prepare themselves. Knowing the land better than their enemies, they are able to take up better positions and expose flaws in the Italian army's tactics. Taytu personally leads a battalion of 5,000 infantry and 600 cavalry to the battlefront. She instructs more than 12,000 women in the camps to fill jugs of water for the soldiers, whom she inspires to fight until the end. It takes just a few hours for Taytu and Menelik's forces to destroy the Italian invasion.

Special empress

The Battle of Adwa ends the war. In a new peace treaty, Italy accepts it does not control Ethiopia. Taytu is celebrated as a hero of the conflict. Her leadership and bravery were crucial at a time when her country perhaps faced its end. As a result, Ethiopia becomes one of two African countries to successfully resist colonization by a European power. Menelik suffers a stroke in 1909, and Taytu takes over as ruler for a short while. Menelik dies in 1913, and Taytu follows him in 1918.

The Battle of Adwa

This painting (by an anonymous artist) of the Battle of Adwa hangs in Addis Ababa, Ethiopia. Taytu Betul and Menelik II look on from horseback as the Ethiopian and Italian armies clash in the field.

Young performer

Born into poverty, Josephine grows up in St. Louis, Missouri, US. She leaves home as a teenager and earns a living as a street performer. By the age of 16, Josephine has toured the US with The Jones Family Band (a group of street performers) and The Dixie Steppers (an all-Black travelling group).

1906...

Broadway debut

Josephine auditions for a role in the musical comedy *Shuffle Along* on Broadway (the hub of the US theatre world). Initially rejected for a role after being told she is "too dark" and "too skinny", she successfully auditions again, and dances in the show for a year.

1922...

Living in harmony

In order to show that different people from all walks of life can live in harmony, Josephine adopts 12 children from around the world, including Japan, Colombia, and Côte d'Ivoire (Ivory Coast). They live with her in her château (country house) in Dordogne, southwest France. She calls her adopted children the "Rainbow Tribe".

1953...

Protest

Though based in France, Josephine goes on several tours in the US. There, she boycotts (protests against) segregated clubs and concert venues. She refuses to perform in venues that stop Black people from buying tickets, or that turn Black ticket-holders away. She retires from the stage in 1956 but continues to perform occasionally.

1951...

1963...

Civil Rights

Josephine is one of the only women to speak during the March on Washington, D.C., organized by African American groups seeking to end repression, segregation, and discrimination. The peaceful protests help to spur the passing of the Civil Rights Act, which improves the lives of African Americans across the country.

1973

Return to performing

Five years after her last appearance on stage, Josephine appears in a run of sell-out shows, including a performance at Carnegie Hall in New York that earns her a standing ovation. She receives positive reviews for her performance.

1975

Final show

Josephine celebrates 50 years since her first appearance in Paris by performing in a revue show at the Bobino Theatre in Paris. She dies during the show's run. More than 20,000 people in Paris pay their respects and celebrate her life.

Beyoncé (b.1981)

American singer, songwriter, and actor Beyoncé Knowles led the girl group Destiny's Child before starting a solo career. A string of successful albums and tours have followed. Beyoncé celebrated what would have been Baker's 100th birthday by performing live in an outfit modelled on one of Baker's famous dresses.

Follow-up shows

After the success of *Shuffle Along*, Josephine goes on to play a leading role as a clown in *The Chocolate Dandies*, a musical stage show about horse racing in a small town. She goes on to work as a performer at the Plantation Club theatre restaurant in Harlem, New York.

Moving to Paris

At the Plantation Club, she meets Caroline Dudley Reagan, the wife of a US diplomat in Paris, France. Reagan invites her to join a theatre group there. Josephine moves to Paris, where she performs with the dance group *La Revue Nègre*. She performs her most famous dance routine, *Danse Sauvage* ("Wild Dance").

Movie success

Josephine's performances catapult her into roles in the French film industry. She is the first African American to star in major movies, including *Siren of the Tropics* (1927), a silent film telling the story of a young girl in love, and *Zou Zou* (1934), the tale of a man accused of murder.

A SCENE FROM *SIREN OF THE TROPICS* (1927)

1924...

1925...

1926...

Back in America

Josephine returns to the US to perform with the Ziegfeld Follies (a music and dance act). Though she is a huge star in Europe, she finds life difficult in the US due to racism. While in the US, she resists racial segregation (enforced separation of people by race) by refusing to perform for audiences in theatres with segregated seating.

Secret agent

While on tour during World War II, Josephine works as a spy. She passes on secrets about German troop movements written on music scores to the French Resistance (anti-Nazi movement). After the war, Josephine becomes the first American woman to be honoured by the French government for her actions during the war.

Superstar

Acting in films including *Princess Tam Tam* (1935), Josephine becomes one of the most famous Black superstars in Europe. But, during this period Black actors have limited choices in the roles they play, and many of the roles she is offered portray negative stereotypes of Black people.

1939...

1936...

1935...

Josephine Baker

One of the most well-known African American entertainers, Josephine Baker (1906–1975) gained international fame through dancing, singing, and acting in Europe. Though she faced discrimination in both the US and Europe, Josephine used her fame to fight prejudice, and even worked as a spy during World War II.

Desmond Tutu (b.1931)
A South African religious leader, activist, and Nobel Peace Prize winner, Desmond Tutu used non-violent methods to campaign against apartheid. He coined the term "Rainbow Nation" in reference to post-apartheid South Africa, which was to be for people of every colour and ethnicity.

1918	1934...	1948	1952	1961	1961...	1964...

Mvezo
Rolihlahla Mandela is born in Mvezo, a small village in eastern South Africa, and spends his boyhood herding cattle. His teacher gives him the English name "Nelson".

Education
Nelson attends a missionary school. In defiance of his headmaster's teaching of the superiority of British culture and government, he grows interested in African history and politics.

Apartheid
The government brings in the apartheid ("separateness") policy. These are a series of racist laws that discriminate against Black South Africans, who make up the vast majority of the population.

Arrest
Nelson becomes one of the leaders of the ANC (African National Congress) and the anti-apartheid cause, speaking at rallies to tens of thousands of people. He is arrested and put in prison for a short time.

In disguise
Disguising himself as a chauffeur to avoid the police, Nelson drives around the country holding secret meetings and arranging for the ANC to strike.

Taking up arms
The government makes it impossible to peacefully protest against apartheid. Nelson helps to set up a resistance group. He is arrested and imprisoned, and then sentenced to life in prison for further crimes in 1964.

Imprisonment
Prison conditions are terrible. Nelson sleeps on a straw mat and carries out hard physical labour. Global opposition to Nelson's imprisonment grows as many see him as an inspirational figure who stands against ingrained racist policies.

Nelson Mandela

A revolutionary activist, Nelson Mandela (1918–2013) led the movement against apartheid – racist laws that discriminated against Black South Africans. His struggle for equality for Black South Africans resulted in him spending 27 years in prison, but when he was freed, he became South Africa's first ever Black head of state.

Mandela's cell

Mandela spent 18 of his 27 years in jail imprisoned at Robben Island, off the coast of Cape Town in South Africa. This photo was taken when he revisited his old cell in 1994, the year he became president of the country.

1989...   1994   1995   1996...   1999...   2013

Election

A multiracial general election is held – the first of its kind in South Africa. The ANC are victorious and Nelson becomes president – a result unthinkable during apartheid.

Truth and Reconciliation

As president, Nelson aims to bring peace to his nation. The Truth and Reconciliation Commission is set up so that both perpetrators and victims under the apartheid era can meet and talk openly. Nelson meets with, and forgives, senior apartheid-era politicians.

Retirement

After retiring, Nelson spends much of his time working on rural development, school construction, and bringing awareness to the HIV/AIDS crisis.

The end of apartheid

F.W. de Klerk comes to power in 1989 and ends the policy of apartheid. He also quashes Nelson's sentence, freeing him in February 1990. Nelson is awarded the Nobel Peace Prize in 1993.

Welfare

Nelson's government increases welfare spending to assist poor citizens, including grants for disability and child maintenance. Nelson donates a third of his monthly wage to help disadvantaged children.

Death

Nelson passes away at the age of 95. Three days after his death, South Africa dedicates a national day to mourn the leader referred to as "the Father of the Nation".

Maya Angelou

Acclaimed writer and poet Maya Angelou (1928–2014) was one of the greatest writers of the 20th century. She is best known for *I Know Why the Caged Bird Sings,* her vivid account of her childhood in the southern US. She was also a poet, dramatist, actor, and an activist for civil rights for African Americans.

1928
"I was born in St. Louis but lived there just for a few minutes in my life".
Interview with CNN (2011)
Maya is born Marguerite Annie Johnson in St. Louis, Missouri. Her parents separate when she is three. Maya and her brother Bailey are sent to live with their grandmother in Arkansas. Bailey nicknames Marguerite "Maya".

1931
"It was awful to be Negro and have no control over my life".
I Know Why the Caged Bird Sings (1970)
In Arkansas, Maya faces racial discrimination and prejudice for the first time. She finds this extremely difficult to deal with.

1935
"In times of strife and extreme stress, I was likely to retreat to mutism".
Interview with the Smithsonian Magazine (2003)
Maya returns briefly to her mother in St. Louis. While there, she is assaulted by her mother's boyfriend. Maya tells people what he did. When her mother's boyfriend is later killed, Maya believes her words have caused his death, and she stops speaking (becomes mute). She is mute for the next five years.

1941
"Her voice slid in and curved down through and over the words. She was nearly singing".
Describing her teacher reading from Charles Dickens in I Know Why the Caged Bird Sings (1970)
Maya lives with her grandmother. A teacher, Mrs Flowers, helps her talk again and inspires a love of literature. Aged 14, she moves to California, living once more with her mother. She studies dance and drama.

1961
"If the heart of Africa remained elusive, my search for it had brought me closer to understanding myself and other human beings".
All God's Children Need Travelling Shoes (1986)
Maya and her son travel to Egypt with South African civil-rights activist Vusumzi Make. The following year, Maya and her son move on to Ghana, where she lives for three years. She involves herself fully in African culture and politics.

Late 1950s
"A Black person grows up in this country... knowing that racism will be as familiar as salt to the tongue".
Interview for the American Academy of Achievement (1997)
Maya travels to New York. She meets African American authors, and joins The Harlem Writers Guild (who help African American writers develop their skills). She hears civil rights leader Martin Luther King Jr. speak. Maya begins to campaign for justice for African American people.

1945
"All my work, my life, everything is about survival... one must not be defeated".
Conversations with Maya Angelou (1989)
At 17, Maya gives birth to her son Clyde "Guy" Johnson. She is a single parent. Maya and Guy move to San Diego, where she works as a waitress and dancer. She marries a man named Tosh Angelos in 1951, and she changes her surname to Angelou. Their relationship ends after three years.

1944
"He asked me, 'Why do you want the job?' I said 'I like the uniforms... and I like people.' And so I got the job".
Interview with Oprah Winfrey (May 2013)
Maya becomes the first female African American cable car conductor in San Francisco. Her mother tells her that, because she is Black, she will have to work much harder than her colleagues in order to keep her job.

1969

"I've **always written**. There's a journal which I kept from about nine years old".

Interview with the Smithsonian Magazine (2003)

Urged on by friends, Maya turns her memories into a book, *I Know Why the Caged Bird Sings*. It is a vivid account of an African American childhood. The novel is wildly successful.

1978

"You may trod me in the very dirt, But still, like dust, **I'll rise**".

And Still I Rise (1978)

Maya's third volume of poetry, *And Still I Rise*, is published. It contains some of her best-loved lines and most famous poems.

1993

"Give birth again, to the **dream**".

From "On the Pulse of Morning" (1993)

She becomes a global icon when she delivers her poem "On the Pulse of Morning" at the inauguration of President Bill Clinton. It speaks about America, and Maya's feelings on the good and bad aspects of American life.

2014

"I'll **probably be writing** when the Lord says, 'Maya, Maya Angelou, it's time'".

Interview with Time Magazine (2013)

Maya dies at the age of 86. She had been writing right up until her death. Tributes pour in from a wide array of people – from media stars, such as Oprah Winfrey, to US presidents, including Bill Clinton and Barack Obama.

1963

RIOTS

11 May
Birmingham riots

A protest following a night of bombings targeted at civil rights leaders turns into eight days of riots in Birmingham, Alabama. Local police respond violently, stunning the country. Media coverage of the riots sparks a national debate.

28 August
"I have a dream"

At the end of a march attended by 250,000 people in Washington, D.C., civil rights leader Martin Luther King Jr. delivers his famous speech from the steps of the Lincoln Memorial. King's powerful words convince many Americans that now is the time for change.

1964

BALLOT OR BULLET?

3 April
Malcolm X gives speech

Activist and religious leader Malcolm X gives a fiery speech in which he promotes change by any means necessary, whether the ballot box or the bullet. Rivals assassinate him in 1965.

FREEDOM SUMMER

June
Register to vote

In Mississippi, thousands of volunteers work together to register as many African American voters as possible. The volunteers face harassment and intimidation.

Equal rights

2 July
1964 Civil Rights Act

After a summer of protests, the US government proposes legislation to end segregation in public places and give everyone equal access to jobs regardless of a person's race, colour, or religion. The act is signed into law by President Lyndon B. Johnson.

7–25 March 1965

Selma

March in Alabama

With Martin Luther King Jr., thousands of marchers walk 80 km (50 miles) from Selma, Alabama to Montgomery, the state capital. The march leads to the passing of the Voting Rights Act in August 1965.

1968

VIOLENCE

4 April
Luther King Jr. shot

A sniper assassinates Martin Luther King Jr. in Memphis, Tennessee. Shock spreads quickly, and riots break out in several US cities. Pressure is put on Congress to pass the legislation that King fought for.

EQUAL ACCESS

11 April
1968 Civil Rights Act

Congress signs this act to give everyone fair and equal access to housing. The impact of civil rights legislation like this is huge, but the march for equality continues.

Selma

The march from Selma to Montgomery was organized to draw attention to the difficulties African Americans faced when registering to vote. Although African Americans had the right to vote, state officials tried to stop them registering. Registration offices were rarely open and officials forced Black people to complete unnecessary literacy tests, fill in long forms, and pay fees.

1929...
Special name
At birth, Martin is named Michael King, in honour of his father, a church pastor in Atlanta, Georgia. When Michael Jr. is five, his father changes both his own and his son's name to "Martin Luther", after the 16th-century German religious reformer.

1944...
BRIGHT STUDENT
From an early age, Martin displays a talent for public speaking and debating. He enrols at Morehouse College as an early admission student aged 15. He receives a bachelor of arts degree and goes on to study theology (the study of God and religious belief). During his youth, he often feels humiliated by the discrimination that he and his family and friends experience on a daily basis.

1946
Moore's Ford Lynchings
Four young African Americans are murdered by a white mob in Martin's home state, an event known as the Moore's Ford Lynchings. Martin writes a letter to Atlanta's most popular newspaper. In his letter, Martin emphasises that African Americans "are entitled to the basic rights of American citizens" — something repeatedly denied them.

1948
Following his father
Martin decides he wants to become a Christian minister and delivers his first sermon from the pulpit of his father's church, aged 18. The congregation votes to make him a minister and he is ordained, becoming an associate minister.

1953
MARRIAGE
Early in 1952, Martin is introduced to Coretta Scott. Two weeks later, he writes to his mother that he has "met his wife". A year later, Coretta and Martin marry, with his father conducting the service.

1955
Rosa Parks
An African American woman, Rosa Parks, is arrested in Montgomery, Alabama for breaking the law by refusing to give up her seat on a bus for a white man. In response, Martin organizes a year-long boycott of the city's buses. It ends when the US Supreme Court rules that segregation laws are illegal.

Civil rights
The ideas behind the US Civil Rights Movement were around for a while, but the movement really took hold in the mid-1950s. Many people fought for African American rights, and to bring about equality.

Septima Poinsette Clark (1898–1987)
A civil rights activist, Septima Poinsette Clark was instrumental in founding nearly 1,000 citizenship schools, which contributed to helping African Americans register to vote.

Shirley Chisholm (1924–2005)
Shirley Chisholm was the first Black woman to be elected to the US Congress. She campaigned for racial and gender equality.

Malcolm X (1925–1965)
Like Martin Luther King Jr., African American activist Malcolm X supported Black Americans' efforts to empower themselves, but didn't believe in the racial integration that King wanted.

1957
Peaceful protest
Following the success of the bus boycott, Martin travels around the US, fighting for civil rights through peaceful protest. He is now the nation's foremost speaker for African American rights. He helps to establish the Southern Christian Leadership Conference, an organization working to achieve equality for African Americans in all areas of US life.

1960
Prison
Martin takes part in a non-violent anti-segregation protest in which he and other protestors occupy a segregated Atlanta department store and refuse to leave. As a result, Martin is arrested. He is sentenced to four months of hard labour in prison.

1963
"I HAVE A DREAM"
While in prison, Martin writes his "Letter From Birmingham Jail", in which he defends non-violent resistance against racism. When released, he delivers his "I Have a Dream" speech to 250,000 people at the Lincoln Memorial in Washington, D.C. – where he calls for a better future for all Americans by ending segregation.

July 1964
Civil Rights Act
The Civil Rights Movement enjoys a huge victory when the Civil Rights Act is signed into law by President Lyndon B. Johnson. It makes any kind of discrimination or segregation on the basis of race illegal.

Oct 1964
Nobel Peace Prize
Time magazine names Martin "Man of the Year". He is also awarded the Nobel Peace Prize for his resistance against racial prejudice in the US. At 35, Martin is the youngest person at the time to have received the award.

1967
Economic justice
Martin reveals his plans for a mass protest. Named the Poor People's Campaign, the movement is intended to bring about economic justice: the idea that everybody should have access to the basic things they need to live. This protest will include people of all walks of life from across the US.

1968
ASSASSINATION
Martin does not live to see the protest. He delivers a speech called "I've Been to the Mountaintop". Towards the end, he talks of the possibility of his untimely death as a result of speaking out about racial issues. The next day, Martin is fatally shot by an assassin.

Martin Luther King Jr.

An activist and a Christian minister, Martin Luther King Jr. (1929–1968) was one of the leaders of the Civil Rights Movement of the 1950s and 1960s, which campaigned for the rights of African Americans. A believer in non-violent protest, his work helped to tear down racial segregation (separation), then a part of the law, and inspire generations of activists seeking a fairer and more equal society.

"Now is the time to make real the promises of democracy".
Martin Luther King Jr.
"I Have a Dream" speech (1963)

The "I Have a Dream" speech

In just 17 minutes, Martin Luther King Jr.'s speech at *The March on Washington for Jobs and Freedom* eloquently explained what the Civil Rights Movement was about, and the kind of change it wanted. With the repeated refrain of "I have a dream..." he gave all Americans – not just those within the Civil Rights Movement – a glimpse of a hopeful future where people will "not be judged by the colour of their skin but by the content of their character". His words on 28 August 1963 – heard by 250,000 people at the march and by many hundreds of thousands more on TV – have continued to inspire generations of people around the world.

Nina Simone

African American musician, songwriter, and activist Nina Simone (1933–2003) enchanted generations with her talent. She also raised awareness about, and campaigned for, civil rights for African Americans, often using her music to explore the realities of life for African Americans of her era.

> **"How can you be an artist and not reflect the times?"**
> **Nina Simone,** *from an interview* **(1960s)**

A musical talent
Eunice Kathleen Waymon is born in North Carolina, US. She learns to play the piano at an early age, and it soon becomes clear that she has a talent for the instrument. She begins to play the piano regularly during church services.

Classical music
Word of Eunice's talent spreads. She meets a pianist called Muriel Mazzanovich. Mazzanovich begins teaching Eunice, focussing on the music of classical pianists such as Johann Sebastian Bach and Ludwig van Beethoven.

Early protest
After years of practice, Eunice is due to perform her first classical recital, but her parents are forced to give up their seats to white audience members. Displaying an early sign of her stance against racial segregation and inequality, Eunice refuses to perform until her parents are allowed to sit at the front.

Musical dream
Realizing her talent, Eunice's local community in North Carolina contribute to a fund to pay for her education. After high school, Eunice receives a one-year scholarship to study music at the famous Juilliard School of Music in New York. She is one of the first Black female artists to attend Juilliard.

Heartbreak
Eunice auditions for another scholarship to continue her musical education. Despite a great audition, her application to the Curtis Institute of Music, Philadelphia, is rejected. Eunice feels certain that she is rejected because she is Black. While some argue that this is not the case, she is never given a clear reason why she is not accepted.

1933...

c.1939

1945

1950

1951

Musical pioneers

In their own unique way, each of these artists changed the sound of music and influenced the development of new types of music.

Billie Holiday (1915–1959)

African American Billie Holiday's songs were crucial in the growth of jazz music. Her most famous song "Strange Fruit" is considered one of the first protest songs of the Civil Rights Movement.

Ella Fitzgerald (1917–1996)

An African American singer, Fitzgerald was famous for using her voice to imitate instruments, known as scat singing. She was known as the "Queen of Jazz", a music genre pioneered by African Americans.

Aretha Franklin (1942–2018)

A gifted pianist and singer, African American Franklin recorded her first album aged 14. She blended genres of music and was known as the "Queen of Soul", another another music genre pioneered by African Americans.

NINA PERFORMING IN ALABAMA IN AUGUST 1963

Rally

Nina regularly speaks and performs at civil rights meetings and rallies. Some of the largest are the Selma to Montgomery marches in Alabama, when about 25,000 people walk 80 km (50 miles) to highlight unjust obstructions to African American voting rights. Nina is one of the many performers to inspire protestors to continue marching.

Emotional distress

Nina's career takes a huge toll on her mental health. She is diagnosed with bipolar disorder – which causes big mood swings in sufferers, something Nina struggles with in both her personal life and while performing.

Musical change

Many of her early records are about love, but when four Black schoolgirls are killed in a racially motivated bombing in Alabama, Nina is furious. The tragedy leads to a change in Nina's music as she brings her experiences as an African American into her music.

An icon

In the later years of her life, close friends help Nina get her life and career back on track. Nina tours the world, giving some amazing performances. She dies from cancer at home in France.

Leaving America

After the assassination of many of the US Civil Rights Movement leaders, the momentum and energy of the movement changes. Nina decides to leave the US for Barbados, and spends several years living in countries such as Liberia, Switzerland, and France.

A rising star

Determined to pursue a music career, Eunice gets a job singing and playing piano at a bar in New Jersey. She believes her family will not approve of this, so she adopts the name "Nina Simone" to keep it a secret. Her audience grows, which leads to a record deal in 1957. One of her first recordings is her version of the song "I Loves You, Porgy" (1958). It becomes a hit.

Political awareness

Nina channels her anger over the assassination of the civil rights activist Medgar Evers into some of her most political songs. Her music is banned in some southern states, but Nina continues to use her music to raise awareness of the Civil Rights Movement.

c.1980s

2003

1970...

1965

1964

1963

1954...

1938

Early years

Ellen is born in Monrovia, Liberia. Her father, the son of a Gola chief, is the first indigenous Liberian to take a seat in the country's parliament.

1948...

Moving about

Ellen and James move to the US. She earns a degree in accounting. They return to Liberia two years later, and Ellen pursues a career with the Treasury Department of Liberia. She divorces her husband after suffering abuse from him.

Finance

She begins studying at the College of West Africa, in Monrovia. Ellen marries James Sirleaf in 1955. They will have four sons together.

1961...

1969...

Further education

Ellen returns to the US to complete her education. She earns a diploma in economics from the University of Colorado. In 1971, she obtains a Master's degree in public administration – the study of how governments make their policies work – from Harvard University.

Ellen Johnson Sirleaf speaking at the 2008 United Methodist General Conference in Texas, US.

Minister of Finance

Ellen moves back to Liberia. She becomes Assistant Minister of Finance under President William Tolbert. In 1979 she rises to the position of Minister of Finance.

Arrest, prison, and exile

Ellen returns to Liberia and runs for the senate. She openly criticizes the government, which leads to her arrest and a term of nine months in prison. After her release, she leaves the country again. During her 12-year-long exile, she works for the World Bank and other financial institutions. A bloody civil war breaks out in Liberia from 1989.

Becoming president

Ellen runs in the 2005 election against famous football player George Weah. She wins the election. Early on in her term she begins to work on sorting out the country's debt problems.

Stepping down

Ellen steps down after winning two more terms as president. She continues to provide support to women who want to have a career in politics.

Military coup

President Tolbert is overthrown and killed in a violent military coup (seizure of power) led by Samuel Doe. Ellen is put under house arrest. She is one of just four ministers of Tolbert's government to not be murdered. She flees to the US after her release.

Presidential campaign

The first civil war in Liberia ends in 1996. Ellen returns and runs for president against Charles Taylor. Taylor wins and his government charges Ellen for treason (betraying the country), which forces her back into exile.

Nobel Peace Prize

Ellen is awarded the Nobel Peace Prize. She is praised for her work to bring the period of war in Liberia to an end, and for her campaign to promote the safety of women throughout Africa.

Ellen Johnson Sirleaf

The first woman to become a head of state in Africa, Ellen Johnson Sirleaf (b.1938) was the president of Liberia from 2006 to 2018. As president, she worked to improve the lives of all Liberians. She jointly won the Nobel Peace Prize in 2011 for promoting peace, and improving women's rights in Liberia.

National icons

Just like Ellen Johnson Sirleaf, these politicians overcame difficult circumstances to become leaders. As a result, they have all become national icons.

Joseph Jenkins Roberts (1809–1876)
The first president of Liberia, US-born Roberts was also the first person of African descent to rule his country. After campaigning for Liberian independence, he sought foreign recognition for the country.

Julius Nyerere (1922–1999)
Tanzanian anti-colonial activist and politician Julius Nyerere became president of the country after it achieved its independence from Britain in 1961. His main achievement is leading the country through the early years of independence without violence or racial divisions.

Fatoumata Tambajang (b.1949)
Gambian activist and politician Fatoumata Tambajang has held a number of roles in Gambian politics. She has been a minister of health and social welfare, minister of women's affairs, and was made vice-president of the country in 2017.

Fela Kuti

Nigerian musician and political activist Fela Kuti (1938–1997) used his great musical talent to take on the Nigerian military government in the 1970s and 1980s. He was a pioneer of a new musical genre called Afrobeat, and both his music and activism brought him critical acclaim and international fame.

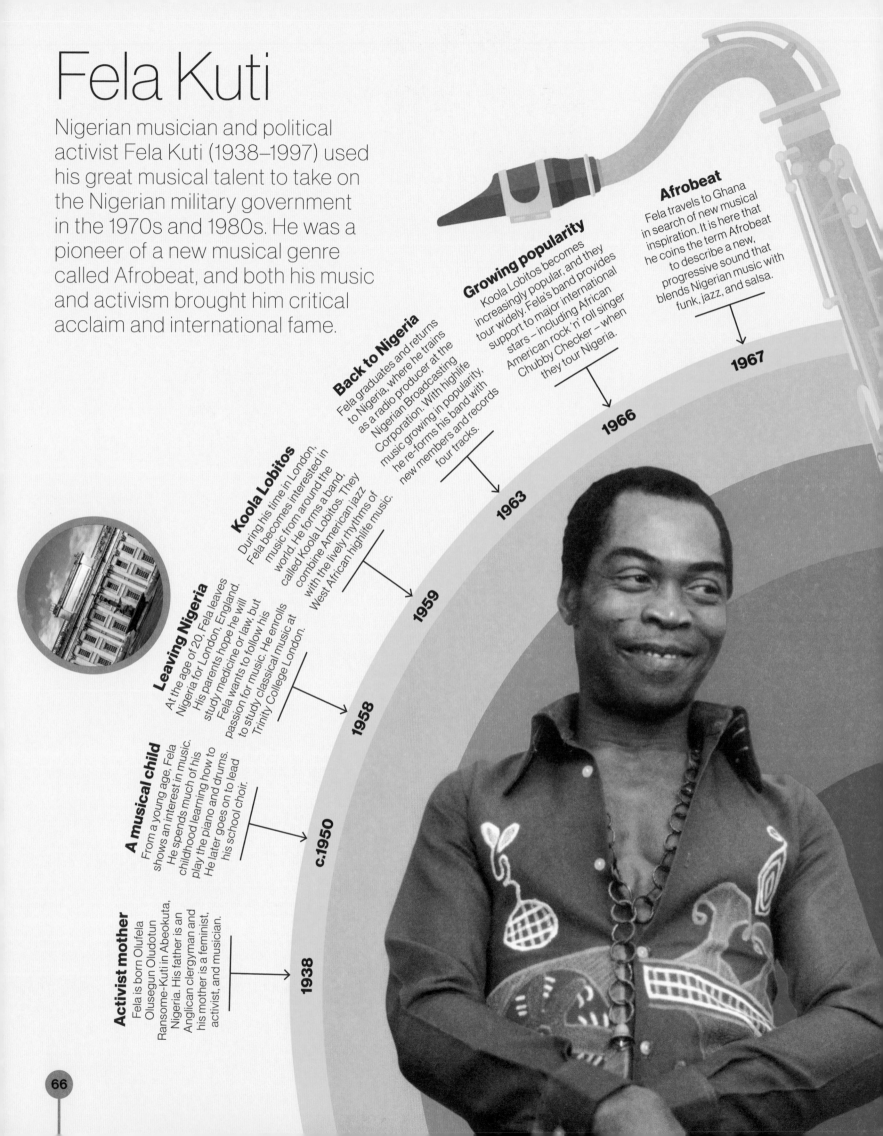

Afrobeat
Fela travels to Ghana in search of new musical inspiration. It is here that he coins the term Afrobeat to describe a new, progressive sound that blends Nigerian music with funk, jazz, and salsa.

1967

Growing popularity
Koola Lobitos becomes increasingly popular, and they tour widely. Fela's band provides support to major international stars – including African American rock 'n' roll singer Chubby Checker – when they tour Nigeria.

1966

Back to Nigeria
Fela graduates and returns to Nigeria, where he trains as a radio producer at the Nigerian Broadcasting Corporation. With highlife music growing in popularity, he re-forms his band with new members and records four tracks.

1963

Koola Lobitos
During his time in London, Fela becomes interested in music from around the world. He forms a band, called Koola Lobitos. They combine American jazz with the lively rhythms of West African highlife music.

1959

Leaving Nigeria
At the age of 20, Fela leaves Nigeria for London, England. His parents hope he will study medicine or law, but Fela wants to follow his passion for music. He enrolls to study classical music at Trinity College London.

1958

A musical child
From a young age, Fela shows an interest in music. He spends much of his childhood learning how to play the piano and drums. He later goes on to lead his school choir.

c.1950

Activist mother
Fela is born Olufela Olusegun Oludotun Ransome-Kuti in Abeokuta, Nigeria. His father is an Anglican clergyman and his mother is a feminist, activist, and musician.

1938

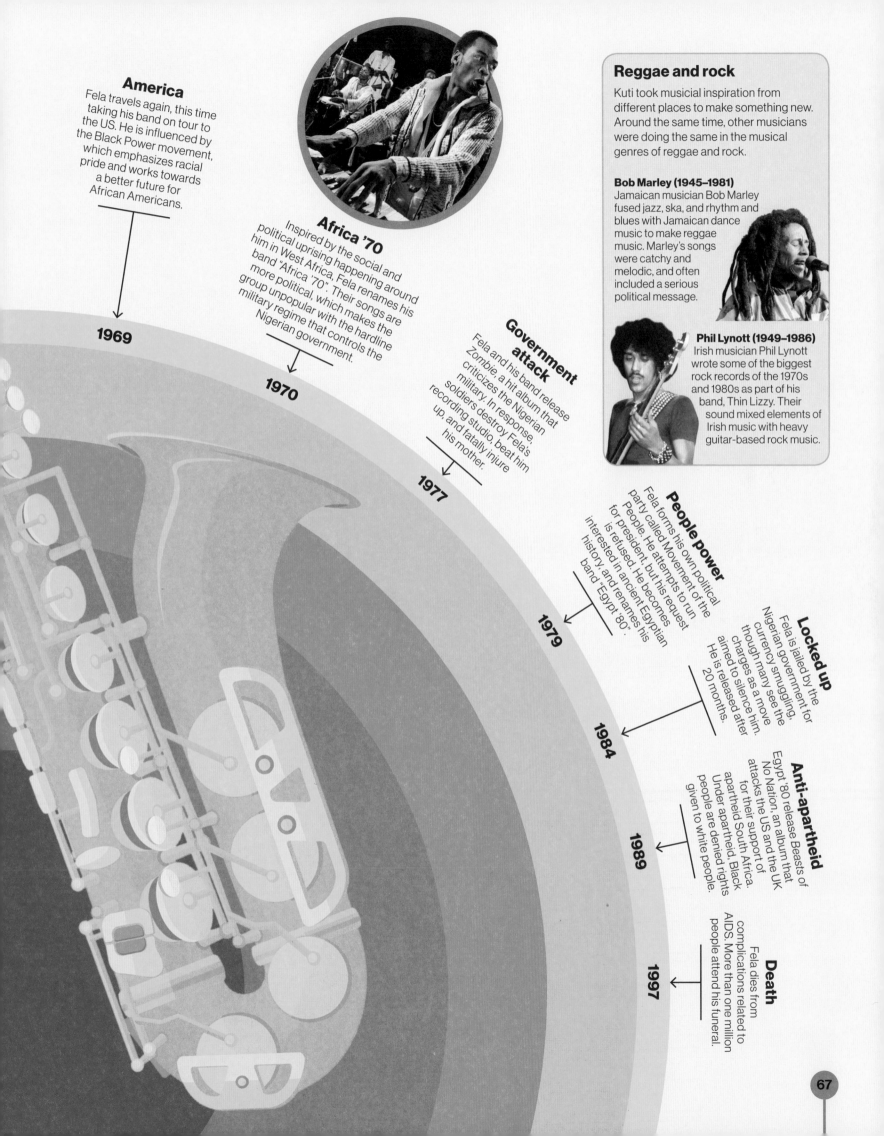

America

Fela travels again, this time taking his band on tour to the US. He is influenced by the Black Power movement, which emphasizes racial pride and works towards a better future for African Americans.

1969

Africa '70

Inspired by the social and political uprising happening around him in West Africa, Fela renames his band "Africa '70". Their songs are more political, which makes the group unpopular with the hardline military regime that controls the Nigerian government.

1970

Government attack

Fela and his band release Zombie, a hit album that criticizes the Nigerian military. In response, soldiers destroy Fela's recording studio, beat him up, and fatally injure his mother.

1977

People power

Fela forms his own political party called Movement of the People. He attempts to run for president, but his request is refused. He becomes interested in ancient Egyptian history, and renames his band "Egypt '80".

1979

Locked up

Fela is jailed by the Nigerian government for currency smuggling, though many see the move aimed to silence him. He is released after 20 months.

1984

Anti-apartheid

Egypt '80 release Beasts of No Nation, an album that attacks the US and the UK for their support of apartheid South Africa. Under apartheid, Black people are denied rights given to white people.

1989

Death

Fela dies from complications related to AIDS. More than one million people attend his funeral.

1997

Reggae and rock

Kuti took musical inspiration from different places to make something new. Around the same time, other musicians were doing the same in the musical genres of reggae and rock.

Bob Marley (1945–1981)
Jamaican musician Bob Marley fused jazz, ska, and rhythm and blues with Jamaican dance music to make reggae music. Marley's songs were catchy and melodic, and often included a serious political message.

Phil Lynott (1949–1986)
Irish musician Phil Lynott wrote some of the biggest rock records of the 1970s and 1980s as part of his band, Thin Lizzy. Their sound mixed elements of Irish music with heavy guitar-based rock music.

Wangari Maathai

Kenyan environmentalist Wangari Maathai (1940–2011) was the founder of the Green Belt Movement, an organization that has arranged the planting of more than 51 million trees in Kenya. She spoke out against Kenya's corrupt government of the 1980s and 1990s, and suffered intimidation and arrest as a result. She won the Nobel Peace Prize in 2004.

> "Until you dig a hole, you plant a tree, you water it and make it survive, you haven't done a thing. You are just talking".
>
> **Wangari Maathai,**
> *Speech at Goldman Environmental Prize awards* **(2006)**

Return to Kenya

Wangari returns to Kenya to continue her studies at the University of Nairobi. Two years later, she receives her doctorate in veterinary anatomy, becoming the first Kenyan woman to earn a PhD. She becomes associate professor at the university, and campaigns for equal treatment for all staff.

Studying in the US

Wangari wins a scholarship to study in the US. She goes on to earn a Master's degree in Biology from the University of Pittsburgh. In the US, Wangari comes across environmentalists demonstrating against their government, inspiring her own later activism.

Nature lover

Growing up on a farm in rural Kenya, Wangari inherits a love of nature from her parents. She excels at school.

1940...   1960...   1969...

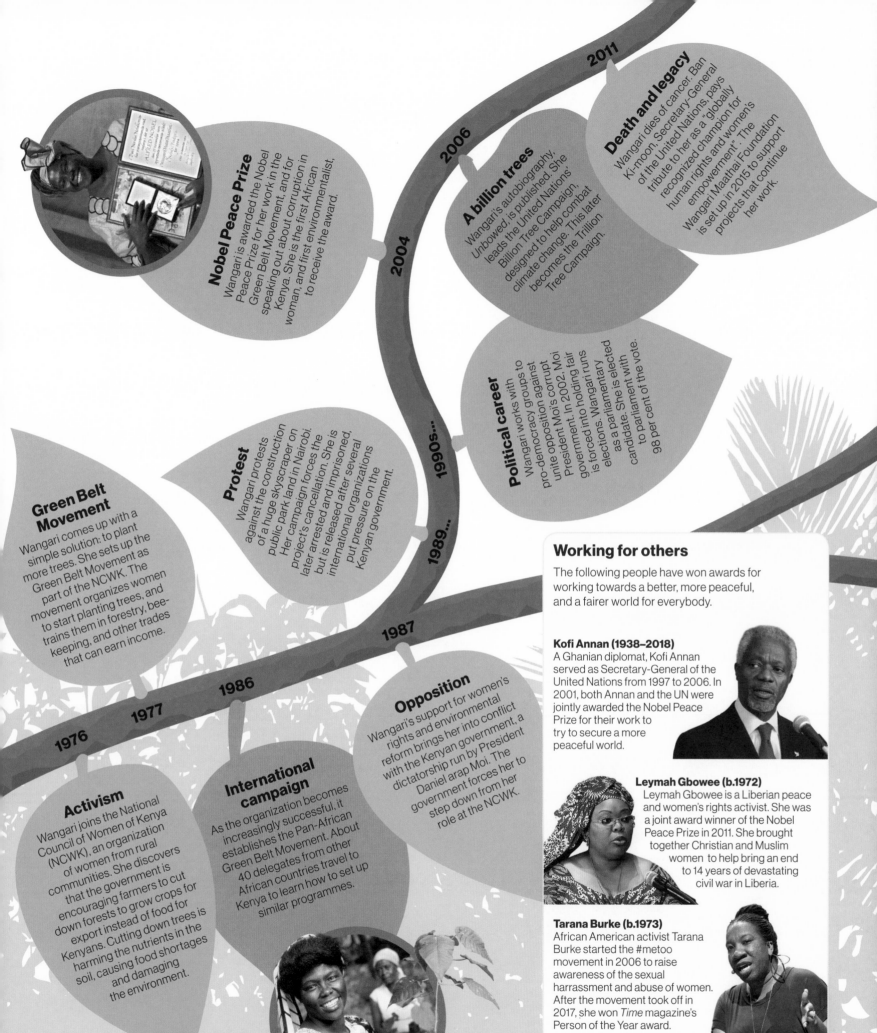

2011

Death and legacy
Wangari dies of cancer. Ban Ki-moon, Secretary-General of the United Nations, pays tribute to her as a "globally recognized champion for human rights and women's empowerment". The Wangari Maathai Foundation is set up in 2015 to support projects that continue her work.

2006

A billion trees
Wangari's autobiography, Unbowed, is published. She leads the United Nations' Billion Tree Campaign, designed to help combat climate change. This later becomes the Trillion Tree Campaign.

Nobel Peace Prize
Wangari is awarded the Nobel Peace Prize for her work in the Green Belt Movement, and for speaking out about corruption in Kenya. She is the first African woman, and first environmentalist, to receive the award.

2004

1990s...

Political career
Wangari works with pro-democracy groups to unite opposition against Moi's corrupt government. In 2002, Moi President is forced into holding fair elections. Wangari runs as a parliamentary candidate. She is elected into parliament with 98 per cent of the vote.

1989...

Protest
Wangari protests against the construction of a huge skyscraper on public park land in Nairobi. Her campaign forces the project's cancellation. She is later arrested and imprisoned, but is released after several international organizations put pressure on the Kenyan government.

Green Belt Movement
Wangari comes up with a simple solution: to plant more trees. She sets up the Green Belt Movement as part of the NCWK. The movement organizes women to start planting trees, and trains them in forestry, bee-keeping, and other trades that can earn income.

1987

1986

1977

1976

Opposition
Wangari's support for women's rights and environmental reform brings her into conflict with the Kenyan government, a dictatorship run by President Daniel arap Moi. The government forces her to step down from her role at the NCWK.

International campaign
As the organization becomes increasingly successful, it establishes the Pan-African Green Belt Movement. About 40 delegates from other African countries travel to Kenya to learn how to set up similar programmes.

Activism
Wangari joins the National Council of Women of Kenya (NCWK), an organization of women from rural communities. She discovers that the government is encouraging farmers to cut down forests to grow crops for export instead of food for Kenyans. Cutting down trees is harming the nutrients in the soil, causing food shortages and damaging the environment.

Working for others

The following people have won awards for working towards a better, more peaceful, and a fairer world for everybody.

Kofi Annan (1938–2018)
A Ghanian diplomat, Kofi Annan served as Secretary-General of the United Nations from 1997 to 2006. In 2001, both Annan and the UN were jointly awarded the Nobel Peace Prize for their work to try to secure a more peaceful world.

Leymah Gbowee (b.1972)
Leymah Gbowee is a Liberian peace and women's rights activist. She was a joint award winner of the Nobel Peace Prize in 2011. She brought together Christian and Muslim women to help bring an end to 14 years of devastating civil war in Liberia.

Tarana Burke (b.1973)
African American activist Tarana Burke started the #metoo movement in 2006 to raise awareness of the sexual harrassment and abuse of women. After the movement took off in 2017, she won *Time* magazine's Person of the Year award.

Muhammad Ali

Boxing champion Muhammad Ali (1942–2016) was one of the greatest sportspeople the world has ever seen. Charismatic, witty, and courageous, he was an outspoken advocate for justice and equality, and an important icon for African Americans.

1942

"[My mother] taught us to love people and treat everybody with kindness. She taught us it was wrong to be prejudiced or hate".

Quoted in Muhammad Ali, His Life and Times by Thomas Hauser (1992)

Muhammad is born Cassius Marcellus Clay in Louisville, Kentucky, US. The eldest son of Cassius and Odessa Clay, he is the descendant of enslaved people and grows up in a segregated neighbourhood.

1954

"My bike got stolen and I started boxing, and it was like God telling me that boxing was my responsibility".

Quoted in Muhammad Ali, His Life and Times by Thomas Hauser (1992)

When Cassius has his bike stolen, he tells the policeman, Joe E. Martin, he's going to "whup" the thief. Martin, the organizer of a boxing club, persuades him to learn to box instead.

1964

"Float like a butterfly, sting like a bee. Rumble, young man, rumble".

Before fighting Sonny Liston (1964)

By February 1964, Cassius has won 19 fights without defeat. He is tall, physically imposing, quick, and full of charm, wit, and charisma. At 22, he defeats reigning champ Sonny Liston and is crowned world heavyweight champion for the first time.

1960

"When I won at the Olympics, that sealed it: I was the champ".

Interview with Oprah Winfrey (2001)

Cassius is chosen for the US Olympic boxing team. After winning three bouts in the qualifying round, he wins the gold medal in the final. The world takes notice. He turns professional two months later.

1954

"I never said I was the smartest. I said I was the greatest".

After taking an Army intelligence test (1964)

Young Cassius has dyslexia, which leads him to struggle during his school years. During his six-year career as an amateur boxer, he wins title after title, including the Kentucky Golden Gloves annual competition six times.

1964

"Cassius Clay is a slave name... I am Muhammad Ali, a free name – it means 'beloved of God'".

Statement to the US media (1964)

In March, Cassius announces his conversion to Islam, and changes his name to Muhammad Ali. The US is simmering with racial tension, and his decision turns some white Americans against him.

1967

"If I thought the war was going to bring freedom and equality to 22 million of my people they wouldn't have to draft me, I'd join tomorrow".

Quoted in Redemption Song by Mike Marquseet (1999)

For religious reasons, Muhammad refuses to join the US Army to fight in the Vietnam War. He is arrested, stripped of his world title, and his boxing licence is suspended. He is banned for three years. To millions of African Americans and other oppressed peoples, however, he becomes an unofficial spokesperson.

1971

"We all have to take defeats in life".

Interview on NBC News after losing to Joe Frazier (1971)

In his first big fight after returning to boxing, Muhammad and Joe Frazier compete in "The Fight of the Century" in New York. In the final round, Frazier's left hook knocks Muhammad down but he lifts himself from the canvas to continue fighting. Frazier emerges the victor on points, inflicting Muhammad's first defeat.

1974

"That all you got, George?"

Whispering in the ear of George Foreman during Round 7 of the "Rumble in the Jungle" (1974)

After losing his heavyweight title the year before, Muhammad – now 32 – goes into a clash in Zaire (modern-day DR Congo) against the undefeated champion, George Foreman, as the underdog. A billion people worldwide watch on TV as he downs Foreman in the eighth round and wins with a knockout. It is one of the greatest sporting contests of the 20th century.

2016

"Your soul and your spirit never dies".

TV interview in the UK (1977)

In 1996, Muhammad lights the Olympic cauldron during the opening ceremony of the Olympic Games in Atlanta. Fans are shocked at his frail appearance. He spends much of the following two decades out of the public eye. He dies, aged 74, in Phoenix, Arizona, and is mourned throughout the world.

1984

"Service to others is the rent you pay for your room here on earth".

Interview with Time magazine (1978)

Muhammad retires from boxing in 1981. Three years later, he is diagnosed with Parkinson's disease, a degenerative disease of the brain. He dedicates the rest of his life to helping others.

1975

"He could have whupped any fighter in the world, except me".

After fighting Frazier in Manila (1978)

In Manila, the capital of the Philippines, Muhammad again meets Frazier in a fight of unrelenting aggression. Fearing for their fighter's safety, Frazier's trainers end the fight between rounds 14 and 15. Muhammad wins, but he is also exhausted and is just about to retire from the fight.

Oprah Winfrey

Rising from unrelenting poverty to become the "queen of all media", Oprah Winfrey (b. 1954) is one of the world's most influential people. She was the first African American multi-billionaire and is considered the greatest Black philanthropist (charity-giver) in US history.

Uplifting moments
Oprah's show's new tagline is "Change Your Life TV". In 2010, scientists study the effects of watching uplifting moments from the show, and find that it makes the watchers more inclined to help others.

Academy nomination
Oprah begins acting in films and seeks out roles which reflect her African American heritage. She receives a nomination for an Academy Award for her role as Sofia in the film adaptation of Alice Walker's book *The Color Purple*.

1985

1994

The Oprah Winfrey Show
On the show, Oprah discusses health, politics, and spirituality. Millions of viewers tune in each week to watch regular people and celebrities being interviewed by Oprah. The show is renamed *The Oprah Winfrey Show* in 1986, and runs for 25 seasons. Oprah sets up her own media company, Harpo, also in 1986.

1984...

Radio and TV
Oprah begins announcing the news at the radio station, making her one of the first Black female news anchors in the US. She works her way through local radio and TV stations. Eventually, she begins working on the morning show of a Chicago TV station.

1972...

A new start
Oprah is abused by relatives in Mississippi. She leaves to live with her father in Tennessee, where she excels in her school studies. She begins to work in a local radio station during her final years in high school, and sticks with it into her early years at university.

1962...

Potato-sack dresses
Born in Mississippi, Oprah was named "Orpah" at birth, but people found "Oprah" easier to pronounce. She is raised by her grandmother in rural poverty. They are so poor that Oprah wears dresses made from potato sack fabric. A bright and inquisitive child, she can recite verses from the Bible by heart at three years old.

1954...

Book club

Oprah starts a book segment on her show called "Oprah's Book Club" to motivate her audience to read more often. Books that appear on her reading list top bestseller charts and sell millions of extra copies.

1996

LGBTQ+ support

Another effect of Oprah's show is that it brings stories about LGBTQ+ (lesbian, gay, bisexual, transgender, and queer) communities to the general public. Oprah invites comedian Ellen DeGeneres onto her show to give her a platform to discuss the reaction to Ellen coming out as a lesbian.

1997

Oprah's she-roes

Oprah has spoken of important women – who she calls "she-roes" – that have inspired her life.

Ida B. Wells (1862–1931)

Like Oprah, African American Ida B. Wells survived a traumatic childhood to embark on a career as a journalist. She wrote about the racial politics in the southern US states, and women's right to vote, and she became an early leader of the Civil Rights Movement.

Alice Walker (b.1944)

An African American novelist, activist, and Pulitzer Prize winner. Alice Walker coined the term "womanist" for Black feminists or feminists of colour. Her most famous book is *The Color Purple*, which tells the story of Black women in the American south in the 1930s.

1998...

Oprah's Angels

Oprah sets up Oprah's Angel Network, which provides grants and funding to non-profit organizations. The network raises more than $80 million for charity programs from initial donations. After Hurricane Katrina (which hit the southern coast of the US, and caused 1,200 deaths) in 2005, the organization raised more than $11 million towards relief efforts.

Empowering change

Highlighting the HIV/AIDS crisis among South African children, Oprah travels around the country raising money and giving gifts. Understanding that education is the key to changing lives and enabling positive change in society, she establishes the Oprah Winfrey Leadership Academy for Girls near Johannesburg. It provides educational opportunities for girls from disadvantaged backgrounds.

2007

2008...

Endorsing Obama

Oprah publicly endorses Barack Obama in his run to become US president in 2008. Election experts later credit the move with securing Obama up to 1.6 million extra votes from Oprah's viewers. In 2013, Oprah is awarded the Presidential Medal of Freedom as a result of her significant cultural contributions to society.

Museum exhibit

The National Museum of African American History and Culture opens a year-long special exhibit called "Watching Oprah" that centres around the profound cultural influence Oprah continues to have on the American public through television.

2018...

"People always said that I didn't give up my seat because I was tired, but that isn't true... No, the only tired I was, was tired of giving in".

Rosa Parks, *My Story* **(1992)**

ROSA PARKS

Sparked the Montgomery Bus Boycott

The Montgomery Bus Boycott was a non-violent civil rights campaign that took place from 1955 to 1956 in Montgomery, Alabama, US. It followed the arrest of Rosa Parks (1913–2005), an African American woman who refused to give up her seat on a bus to a white man. Rosa's brave action inspired more than 40,000 African Americans to protest by refusing to take the city's buses. The protest ended when the US Supreme Court finally ordered Montgomery to integrate its bus system.

Abolition and the KKK

In **1865**, the 13th Amendment to the US Constitution was passed, abolishing slavery across the United States. Around 4 million enslaved people were freed. In the same year, a secret society called the "Ku Klux Klan" (KKK) formed. Believing white people to be superior, they terrorized Black people, vandalizing schools and businesses, burning down homes, and violently attacking and murdering thousands of Black people. Legislation was passed to crush the KKK in the early **1870s** but the society saw a huge resurgence in the 1920s and the 1950s.

Jim Crow and civil rights

In **1877**, the first of a set of laws that become known as the "Jim Crow" laws was introduced in the southern states. These laws legalized discrimination against Black people – taking away the right to vote from many, and dictating where they could work, eat, and live. These laws eroded the few rights that Black citizens enjoyed. In **1909**, the NAACP (The National Association for the Advancement of Colored People) was established by a group of African American activists to fight back. Over the next decades, the NAACP played a key part in the development of the Civil Rights Movement. This movement campaigned to outlaw segregation, change voting rights, and oppose discriminatory laws.

Rosa Parks

In **late 1943**, an African American seamstress named Rosa Parks joins her local NAACP branch in Montgomery, Alabama, where she is later elected to be a secretary. She works with the branch president, Edgar Nixon, organizing equal justice campaigns and investigating cases of violence against Black women. By the **1950s**, the growing US Civil Rights Movement has begun to inspire a wave of protests across the southern states, as African Americans start to defy segregation laws. One such protestor is Claudette Colvin, a teenage nurse and member of the local NAACP Youth Council in Montgomery. The bus system in Montgomery is segregated by law – white people sit at the front of the bus, and Black people have to sit at the back. On **2 March 1955**, Colvin refuses to give up her bus seat to a white woman and is arrested. Some local civil rights leaders see the event as a chance to highlight the city's racist bus policy, but in the end they decide that Colvin is too young to represent the struggle. Nine months later, on **1 December**, Rosa Parks boards a bus and takes a seat behind a row filled with white passengers. When the bus stops, a white man boards and finds there are no free seats in the "whites-only" area. The bus driver, James Blake, orders Rosa to give her seat up for the man. She refuses. Police officers board the bus and arrest Rosa. News spreads fast about her arrest. She is released in the evening when her NAACP colleagues bail her out.

Montgomery Bus Boycott

The case angers many. As Rosa is a respected member of her community, Edgar Nixon thinks that the incident could benefit the NAACP. On the night of her arrest, the Women's Political Council, a part of the Civil Rights Movement, prints and circulates flyers to the Black community in Montgomery urging them to boycott (stop using) bus services. On **2 December**, Rosa joins a meeting at the Dexter Avenue Church, where they discuss how to implement a citywide boycott of public transport. The mass boycott begins on **5 December**, with Black taxi drivers lowering their prices to that of a bus ticket in solidarity. However, the boycott causes a backlash. In retaliation, groups of white thugs firebomb activists' houses and many Black churches, and physically attack boycotters. The protest gains national attention and much support from the public. After mounting public pressure, the US Supreme Court upholds a court ruling that segregation on public buses is against the law on **13 November 1956**. The boycott ends, after 381 days, on **20 December 1956**, as the city is finally forced to allow Black people to sit anywhere on public transport.

Life after the boycott

Although the Montgomery Bus Boycott has been successful, many white Americans do not agree with the new laws. Over the next few months, there are shootings of buses and bus passengers, as well as frequent attacks on individuals. Despite this, the Montgomery Bus Boycott has been an important part of the Civil Rights Movement, as it has shown how non-violent protest can bring about change. The NAACP and the wider Civil Rights Movement continues to fight racist laws. They successfully campaign for the passing of the Civil Rights Act of **1964**, which bans discrimination based on race. In **1965**, the Voting Rights Act is passed, which makes practices that prevent African Americans from voting illegal. Rosa Parks continues to campaign for and support civil rights causes right up to her death in **2005**.

Postcolonial Africa

In the 1950s and 1960s, African nations gained independence from colonial rule with varying degrees of success. Although there was freedom in many places, there was also corruption, military coups, civil war, and division among different ethnic groups. However, in the 21st century, optimism is growing, with greater wealth and improving political stability.

Rwandan Genocide

More than a million people of the Tutsi ethnicity in Rwanda are killed by members of the neighbouring ethnic group, the Hutus. The international community fails to stop the genocide (the killing of a large number of people because of their ethnicity).

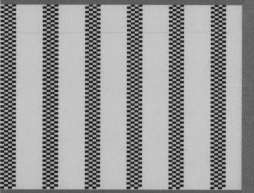

Ghanaian independence

Kwame Nkrumah becomes the country's first independent prime minister after years of British colonial rule. In an emotional speech, he tells tens of thousands of Ghanaians: "your beloved country is free forever".

> ## "In the end, the ballot must decide, not bullets".
> **Angolan politican Jonas Savimbi,** *from a speech* **(1975)**

President Nelson Mandela

After decades of apartheid (racial segregation) in his country, and 27 years of imprisonment for protesting against it, Nelson Mandela is elected the first Black president of South Africa. This ends 300 years of white rule.

1957   **1960...**   **1963**   **1971...**   **1975... 1984...**   **1994**   **1994**

Congo Crisis

The Congo (modern-day Democratic Republic of Congo) dissolves into crisis after becoming independent from Belgium in June 1960. A breakaway state of Katanga exists until the United Nations (UN) intervenes in 1963. The army seizes power in 1965.

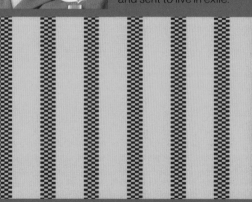

Idi Amin

Ugandan president Amin expels Asian minorities from Uganda and launches an unsuccessful attack against Tanzania. Following eight years of erratic rule, he is overthrown in 1979 and sent to live in exile.

African Unity

Following the independence of many African nations from European rule, the Organization of African Unity is established by 32 African states to encourage and protect Africa's interests.

Ethiopian famine

Decades of war and extreme drought cause agricultural decline, resulting in widespread starvation in Ethiopia. About 1 million die, with many left hungry and poor. Many are forced to leave their homes and resettle elsewhere.

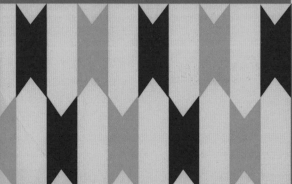
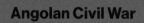

Angolan Civil War

The Republic of Angola, rich in diamonds and oil, becomes independent from Portugal in 1975, but suffers social and economic turmoil when civil war breaks out. This will be one of Africa's longest-running conflicts.

Economic boom

Africa is predicted to have the largest economic growth of any continent over the next decades. Industries such as telecommunications, retail, and banking help the continent to flourish financially.

Kofi Annan

Kofi Annan from Ghana becomes the Secretary-General of the United Nations. He expands the UN's work into protecting the environment, fighting against HIV/AIDS in Africa, and improving human rights.

Election day

Nigeria votes out President Goodluck Jonathan in favour of Muhammadu Buhari. Despite being divided along ethnic, regional, and religious lines, Jonathan is gracious in his defeat to Buhari.

Civil war in Sudan

Civil war begins in the Darfur region of Sudan between rebel groups and the government. Several hundred thousand people are killed and millions flee their homes, in a conflict that remains unresolved today.

Independence for South Sudan

South Sudan votes to break away from Sudan after a civil war between the mainly Christian south and the Arab Muslim north. Much of the world recognizes the new nation, but it remains in crisis, due to its struggling infrastructure.

Life expectancy

Across the continent, life expectancy increases by 9.4 years in just one decade. This is thanks to developments in healthcare, access to medical treatment, and improved governance.

1997   2003   2004   2010   2010   2011   2011   2014...   2015   2016   2017

Prize for Kenya

Wangari Maathai, a Kenyan feminist and environmentalist, receives the Nobel Peace Prize. Her Green Belt Movement teaches women to grow trees in order to improve their living conditions.

Ebola

West Africa experiences the biggest outbreak of the Ebola virus ever known. Thousands die and the economies of many countries are damaged, some of which are still recovering from civil war.

World Cup

The football World Cup comes to South Africa, the first time an African nation has held such a prestigious worldwide event. The tournament is a success, boosting both tourism and South Africa's international image.

Rwandan reform

Rwanda manages to rebuild its economy after its devastating civil war. Life expectancy, the number of children attending primary school, and the amount of money spent on healthcare have all improved.

Robert Mugabe steps down

Robert Mugabe, president of Zimbabwe since 1980, loses his grip on power and resigns after the military take control. He is blamed for economic chaos, preventing political freedom, and the abuse of human rights.

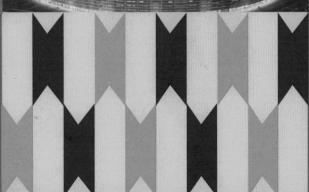

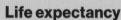

Kwame Nkrumah and Ghanaian Independence

In this photograph, officials from the Ghanaian government carry revolutionary and politician Kwame Nkrumah (1909–1972) aloft to celebrate Ghana's independence from British rule in 1957. Nkrumah led the campaign for independence, and became the country's first president in 1960. He was a supporter of Pan-Africanism, the worldwide movement that aims to strengthen the cultural bonds between all people of African descent. He also helped set up the Organization of African Unity – a political body set up in 1963 that aimed to improve the lives of Africans living on the continent.

Barack Obama

Barack Obama (b.1961) was the first African American to be elected president of the US. A charismatic and gifted speaker, he introduced affordable healthcare, worked to improve the US' reputation abroad, and committed to tackling global warming.

Michelle Obama (b.1964)

Chicago-born lawyer and campaigner Michelle Obama pursued a successful career in law and city administration before becoming First Lady. She has campaigned on issues such as poverty, healthy living, and education, and published a best-selling memoir, *Becoming*, in 2018.

44th US President

Barack runs for the US presidency and campaigns with a message of hope and change. He wins the election and becomes the first African American to become US president. He must hit the ground running as the US is suffering from an economic crisis, with many people losing their jobs, savings, and even homes.

2008...

2009

Nobel Prize winner

The new president is awarded the Nobel Peace Prize for his efforts to strengthen cooperation between nations. Much of his early presidency is spent trying to limit the damage of the economic crisis, and dealing with the wars in Afghanistan and Iraq that started before he became president.

Obamacare

Despite opposition, Barack pushes through the Affordable Care Act, popularly known as "Obamacare". Its aim is to make healthcare available to the poorest US citizens.

2010

Second term

Barack is elected to a second term as president. He makes combating global warming a priority. He signs a major international agreement to reduce carbon emissions, the main contributor to global warming.

2012...

Leaving office

After his second term ends, Barack returns to private life. Both Michelle and Barack agree to write autobiographies. Barack occasionally gives speeches on issues that he worked on during his presidency, such as global warming.

2017...

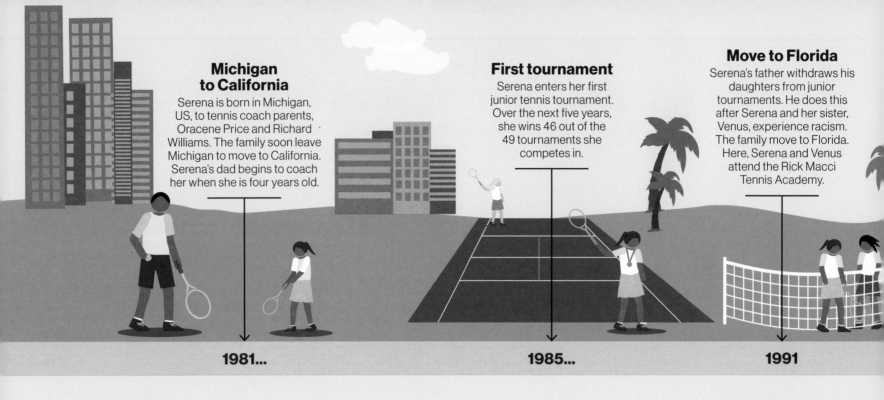

Michigan to California

Serena is born in Michigan, US, to tennis coach parents, Oracene Price and Richard Williams. The family soon leave Michigan to move to California. Serena's dad begins to coach her when she is four years old.

1981...

First tournament

Serena enters her first junior tennis tournament. Over the next five years, she wins 46 out of the 49 tournaments she competes in.

1985...

Move to Florida

Serena's father withdraws his daughters from junior tournaments. He does this after Serena and her sister, Venus, experience racism. The family move to Florida. Here, Serena and Venus attend the Rick Macci Tennis Academy.

1991

Serena Williams

One of the greatest tennis players of all time, Serena Williams (b.1981) has won 73 singles titles, 23 doubles titles, and four gold medals at the Olympic Games. Williams' success is built on her power, agility, and mental toughness.

Tragedy strikes

After suffering from an injured knee for some time, Serena is forced to undergo surgery and takes time off to recover. A month later, her half-sister Yetunde is murdered. Serena does not return to tennis for eight months.

2003...

2004...

On top form

Serena returns to tennis, and wins the Australian Open in 2005. She goes on to win the US Open three years later, and by 2009, she has earned back her spot as the world's number one.

Illness

Doctors discover a blood clot in Serena's lungs. She is forced to take time away from tennis, and it is rumoured that she might retire. Following surgery, her health improves, and she returns to training.

2011

Olympic winner

Serena's return means she does not miss the 2012 Olympic Games in London, UK. She takes home the gold medal for women's singles tennis by beating Maria Sharapova in the final. Her winning streak continues at the US Open, where she wins the title.

2012

Going pro

At the age of 14, Serena decides to dedicate her life to playing tennis professionally. After losing her debut professional match, she takes a break from competing and dedicates herself to training for the next two years.

Making an impact

Serena returns to competitive tennis. Aged 16, she beats professional tennis players Mary Pierce and Monica Seles at the Ameritech Cup, before losing to Lindsay Davenport in the semi-finals. At the end of a great year, she breaks into the top 100 players in the world.

Tennis greats

Over the past century, women's tennis has become one of the world's most popular sports. Its greatest players have become an inspiration to sports fans around the world.

Althea Gibson (1927–2003)

Described as a "forgotten pioneer", Althea Gibson was the first African American tennis player to win a tennis Grand Slam in 1956. She won 11 Grand Slam tournaments over the course of her career.

Venus Williams (b.1980)

Serena's older sister Venus is also a professional tennis player. She has won seven Grand Slam singles titles, and been ranked the world's best player three times.

Naomi Osaka (b.1997)

Naomi Osaka became the world's top female tennis player in January 2019. Though she represents Japan, she grew up in America, and is the daughter of a Japanese mother and a Haitian father. She defeated Serena Williams in the final to win the US Open in 2018, and looks set to dominate the game for years to come.

1995...   **1997**   **1998...**

The "Serena Slam"

Serena wins the four Grand Slam tennis titles – the US Open, the French Open, the Australian Open, and Wimbledon. Her triumph is called the "Serena Slam" in the press. After an unbelievable year, Serena is now the number one player in the world.

Graduation

Serena signs a $12 million business deal with Puma, a sportswear company. A year later, she graduates from high school. Her tennis career goes from strength to strength, and she wins the US Open, her first major title.

2002...

Engagement

Serena gets engaged to American tech business owner Alexis Ohanian. A year later, they marry and Serena gives birth to a girl, Alexis Olympia Ohanian Jr.

Entrepreneur

Serena launches her own women's clothing company, Serena – describing the inspiration behind her designs as "strong women everywhere".

Number one

After losing against Sabine Lisicki at Wimbledon, Serena returns to form at the US Open. She wins the title for the fifth time, and becomes the world's number one player for the sixth time in her career.

2013   **2016...**   **2018...**

LeBron James

Considered by many to be the greatest basketball player of all time, LeBron James (b.1984) made his name playing for the Cleveland Cavaliers and the Miami Heat before moving on to the Los Angeles Lakers. He has been successful wherever he has played, and shows no signs of slowing down.

LeBron's Foundation
Inspired by his experience of growing up in a single-parent household, he sets up the LeBron James Family Foundation. It aims to assist and empower single-parent families and children to succeed in education and daily life. He debuts with the US men's basketball team at the 2004 Olympic Games. They take home bronze medals.

First NBA final
Now captaining the team, LeBron makes his NBA finals debut with the Cleveland Cavaliers. He plays well, averaging 22 points per game across four games, but the team lose to the San Antonio Spurs.

LeBron goes big
After graduating from high school, LeBron decides to become a professional basketball player. He enlists with the National Basketball Association (NBA), and is drafted (chosen) by the Cleveland Cavaliers. He wins the NBA's "Rookie of the Year" award, given to the best new player in the league.

2007

2004

2003

High school success
LeBron continues playing basketball under Walker and youth basketball coach Dru Joyce II. He joins his high school basketball team and leads them to success with three state championship wins.

1999...

Frank Walker
LeBron's life becomes more unstable. He and his mother often move homes, and he misses many days of school. LeBron's mother struggles to find work, and sends him to live with Frank Walker, one of his football coaches. Walker teaches him how to play basketball, and he joins a youth league basketball team.

1994...

American football
LeBron is playing with friends when a youth American football coach, Bruce Kelker, passes by. LeBron tells Kelker that football is his favourite sport. To test LeBron's athleticism, he makes the children race. LeBron wins, and Kelker selects him to play for his youth football team.

1992...

Early life
LeBron Raymone James is born to Gloria Marie James and Anthony McClelland in Akron, Ohio, US. His father is absent for much of his childhood. As a young single mother, Gloria struggles to support their small family and they move often during LeBron's childhood.

1984...

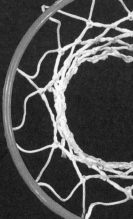

Brilliant basketballers

Basketball was invented in the late 1800s, but grew popular in the mid-20th century when the National Basketball Association (NBA) was set up, and it was made an Olympic sport.

Earvin "Magic" Johnson Jr. (b.1959)

"Magic" Johnson won five NBA championships and three MVP awards with the LA Lakers over 13 seasons in the NBA. Retiring in 1991, Johnson went on to build a business empire.

Michael Jordan (b.1963)

Often considered to be LeBron James' only rival for the title of greatest basketball player ever, Jordan won six NBA championships with the Chicago Bulls and received the NBA MVP award five times.

Tamika Catchings (b.1979)

Tamika Catchings won four Olympic gold medals for the US women's basketball team. She played 14 seasons in the Women's NBA (WNBA), winning the championship in 2012.

Most Valuable Player (MVP)

LeBron keeps improving as a player. He receives the NBA's MVP Award, given to the best-performing player of the season.

2009

Move to Miami

With his contract finished in Cleveland, LeBron becomes a free agent. This means he is able to move to any team that makes him an offer. He decides to join the Miami Heat, where he stays for four years.

2010...

NBA win

In an incredibly successful year, LeBron wins his first NBA championship. Two months later, he wins Olympic gold with the US men's basketball team. The following year, he becomes the youngest player to score 20,000 career points, as he leads the Heat to a second NBA championship. He goes on to win two more MVP awards in Miami.

2012...

Back to Cleveland

LeBron leaves the Miami Heat, and returns to Cleveland to rejoin the Cavaliers. He leads them to the NBA finals, although they lose out to San Francisco's Golden State Warriors.

2014

The winning Cavaliers

Desperate to win a first-ever NBA championship for the Cavaliers, LeBron and the team come back to win the finals from being one game to three down against Golden State. For his heroics on the court, LeBron is named MVP again.

2016

LA Lakers

LeBron signs a four-year contract with the Los Angeles Lakers, earning him more than $150 million. He continues to be one of the top performers in the league.

2018...

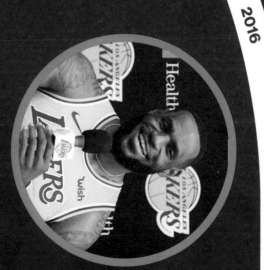

Stormzy

Born Michael Omari, Stormzy is one of England's most successful musicians of the 21st century. In 2017, his debut album, *Gang Signs and Prayer*, became the first grime album to hit No.1 in the UK album charts. A year later, he launched #Merky Books, aimed at discovering new and diverse voices in literature.

College and music

Following his win, Stormzy graduates from high school. He finds college difficult and eventually drops out. He begins an engineering apprenticeship, but becomes swayed by his growing passion for making and performing music.

Unsigned Stars

Both talented and smart, Stormzy does very well in school, but he also continues performing. He competes in Unsigned Stars, an annual competition for up-and-coming rappers, singers, dancers, and poets. He raps his way to victory.

Early days

Michael Omari is born and raised in south London, England. He listens to a wide range of music from an early age, from church gospel to R&B and grime, a type of fast electronic music from London.

1993...   2004...   2011   2012   2013

Rap Academy

Around eleven years old, Michael becomes obsessed with performing after listening to the grime artists Kano and Lethal Bizzle. He goes to his local youth club, Rap Academy, where he invites others to enter into musical battles with him. He starts using the name Stormzy for performances, and begins honing his rapping skills.

Mixtape

Stormzy releases his "168: The Mixtape", a compilation of his music that takes its name from the fact it was recorded in one week (168 hours). Stormzy's profile as a musician really starts to grow.

Black British music

Young Black British musicians have stormed the charts and made huge contributions to British music culture in recent years.

Lady Leshurr (b.1988)
Lady Leshurr is a British rapper, songwriter, singer, and producer. In 2015, her freestyle "Queen's Speech" raps went viral, and a year later, she won a MOBO Award. Leshurr is a mental-health advocate and has established numerous youth clubs.

Krept (b.1990) and Konan (b.1989)
Krept and Konan are a British rap duo. In 2017, they became the first act to have two mixtapes in the UK top 10 album chart. In 2018, they opened their dessert restaurant, Crepes and Cones. Passionate about charity work, their Positive Direction Foundation works to inspire creativity in young people.

Dave (b.1998)
Dave is a British rapper, singer, songwriter, actor, and producer. In 2018, he won the Ivor Novello Award for his politically-charged song, "Question Time", and a year later, he won the BRIT Award for his album, *Psychodrama*. Dave is also a self-taught classical pianist.

Dreamers Disease

Stormzy quits his apprenticeship to focus fully on music. He releases *Dreamers Disease* – a seven-track mini-album. He later wins Best Grime Act at the Music of Black Origin (MOBO) Awards – an annual award show that recognizes achievements in a range of musical genres such as R&B, gospel, hip-hop, and grime.

Debut album

Gang Signs and Prayer, Stormzy's debut full-length album, is released through his own record label, #Merky Records. It becomes the first grime album to reach No.1 in the UK album chart. He wins numerous awards, including Artist of the Year at the BBC Music Awards.

#Merky Books

Stormzy launches his publishing company, #Merky Books, with the aim of focusing on new and exciting authors and poets. His memoir, *Rise Up*, is the first book published, and is a big success. He later performs a freestyle rap at the BRIT Awards, criticizing Prime Minister Theresa May for her inaction in response to the Grenfell Tower fire – a tragedy that claimed the lives of more than 70 people in 2017.

Helping others

In the aftermath of the Black Lives Matter protests, Stormzy pledges to donate £10 million over the coming decade to UK charitable organizations working to tackle racial inequality, reform the legal system, and encourage Black empowerment in the UK.

2014 **2015** **2016** **2017** **2018** **2019** **2020...**

Shut Up

Stormzy performs an improvised freestyle rap, "Shut Up", over an instrumental track by Ruff Sqwad, an English grime group. The song enters the UK singles chart at No.18, his first success in the charts.

Hiatus

Stormzy criticizes the BRIT Award panel – who give awards for achievements in the British music industry – for not recognizing the grime music genre. After releasing a song titled "Scary", Stormzy goes on a year-long hiatus from social media in order to concentrate working on his debut full-length album.

Huge success

"Vossi Bop", the first track to be taken from Stormzy's second album, *Heavy Is the Head*, reaches No.1 in the UK singles chart. Later, Stormzy becomes the first grime artist to headline the Pyramid stage at Glastonbury Festival – the biggest stage of the largest music festival in the UK. His performance is widely praised.

Mari Copeny

Perhaps better known as "Little Miss Flint", Amariyanna "Mari" Copeny (b.2007) has campaigned to raise awareness of the poisioned water supply in her hometown of Flint, Michigan, US. In 2016, at the age of eight, she wrote to US President Barack Obama to tell him that Flint's water supply was contaminated with lead, causing people to become ill. President Obama visited Flint and soon declared the situation a Federal emergency, and allocated government money to begin to fix the problem. Copeny has continued to raise awareness and funds to help the people of Flint, and she has also spoken out on issues affecting school children and immigrants.

Marley Dias

Marley Dias (b.2005) noticed that most stories in her school books were about, as she explained, "white boys and dogs". This caused her to launch a social media campaign to call for more books with Black girls as main characters in 2015. Her campaign, #1000BlackGirlsBooks, aimed to collect 1,000 books to donate to Black girls, while also raising awareness about the lack of diversity in children's literature more generally. The campaign was a success on both fronts. Tens of thousands of books were donated across the world, and Dias has encouraged many publishers to create new books written by or featuring Black girls, including Dias' own first book.

Black history stars

From leaders, politicians, and activists, to actors, writers, and athletes, Black people from all over the world have made crucial and lasting contributions to the modern world. Here are just a few more notable people, all of whom have made groundbreaking achievements, often while encountering racism and inequality in their daily lives.

Nanny of the Maroons (c.1686–c.1740s)

Nanny was the leader of the Windward Maroons, a community of formerly enslaved people in Jamaica. She led the Maroons in their guerilla war against the British forces that had colonized the island. Though the facts of many parts of her life have been lost over time, she has become a national icon in Jamaica.

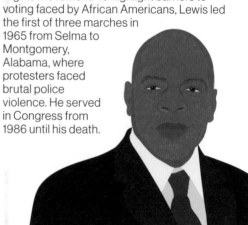

James Baldwin (1924–1987)

A key figure in the US Civil Rights Movement, African American writer and activist James Baldwin travelled the country lecturing against racial inequality and attending protest marches. Drawing on his own experiences as a gay Black man, Baldwin's writings explored ideas about race, class, and sexuality.

Frantz Fanon (1925–1961)

Frantz Fanon was a Martinique-born psychiatrist whose work focused on the psychological impact of colonialism on colonized people. His work blended historical analysis, philosophy, psychology, the Négritude movement of Aimé Césaire, and observations from his own life and experiences. He inspired many Black revolutionaries to seek liberation from their colonizers.

John Lewis (1940–2020)

African American activist and politician John Lewis was an important leader in the US Civil Rights Movement. To highlight barriers to voting faced by African Americans, Lewis led the first of three marches in 1965 from Selma to Montgomery, Alabama, where protesters faced brutal police violence. He served in Congress from 1986 until his death.

Black Panthers (est.1966)

The Black Panthers campaigned against police violence against African Americans, and fought for better housing, employment, and justice for all Black people. Its 2,000 members – two-thirds of which were women – offered free meals and health clinics in African American communities until government efforts to discredit the organization led to its decline.

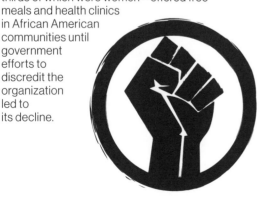

Jay-Z (b.1969)

Born in New York, African American rapper Jay-Z released his first album *Reasonable Doubt* in 1996. He has since sold more than 50 million albums worldwide, and broken a string of records. His rapping is based on clever wordplay and a laid-back vocal style. He is also a successful entrepreneur.

Janelle Monáe (b.1985)

Janelle Monáe is an award-winning African American singer and actor. She began releasing music in 2007. She uses her platform as a musician to express support for the Black Lives Matter movement and the LGBTQ+ community, and to campaign for better gun control in the US.

Paul Robeson
(1898–1976)

Paul Robeson blended his interests in singing, acting, and activism together throughout his life. In 1943, he became the first African American to lead a Broadway production, when he took the lead role in the Shakespeare play *Othello*. It became the most successful Shakespeare production in Broadway history.

Aimé Césaire
(1913–2008)

Poet and politician Aimé Césaire was born on the Caribbean island of Martinique, then a French colony. Césaire was a founder of the Négritude movement. It brought together writers, intellectuals, and politicians who criticized colonialism, and called for greater recognition of Black history and culture.

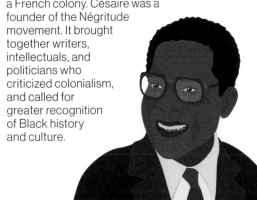

Katherine Johnson
(1918–2020)

African American mathematician Katherine Johnson overcame racism and sexism to become key to the success of the US space program. Her important work helped put the first US astronaut into space, and the first-ever humans on the moon. She worked at NASA for 33 years making the complex calculations required for missions into space.

Angela Davis
(b.1944)

Author, activist, philosopher, and university professor Angela Davis has spoken up against injustice throughout her life. She joined the Communist Party in 1969 and also was a part of the feminist and Black Panther movements. Davis continues to lecture at many universities today, discussing issues including prison abolition.

Marsha P. Johnson
(1945–1992)

US gay rights activist and drag queen Marsha P. Johnson campaigned against discrimination toward LGBTQ+ people. Often seen wearing a crown of flowers, Johnson led protests during the 1969 Stonewall Uprisings in which the LGBTQ+ community of New York stood up against police brutality.

Doreen Lawrence
(b.1952)

After British police failed to solve her son Stephen's murder by racists in London, England, in 1993, Jamaican-born Doreen Lawrence spent years fighting for justice. A 1999 inquiry into the investigation revealed the police were institutionally racist, leading to widespread reform. Lawrence continues to support and campaign for justice for the victims of racism.

Usain Bolt
(b.1986)

Jamaican sprinter Usain Bolt is the planet's fastest man, holding the world record time of 9.58 seconds for running 100m in 2008. Bolt made history winning the 100m and 200m titles at three consecutive Olympic Games, and holds eight Olympic gold medals in total. He retired in 2017.

Simone Biles
(b.1997)

The most successful US gymnast, with 25 world championship medals to her name, Simone Biles led the US female gymnastics team to first place at the Olympics in Rio de Janeiro, Brazil, in 2016, while also winning individual medals in the vault, the floor, and the balance beam. Many believe her to be the greatest gymnast ever.

Black Lives Matter
(est.2013)

First set up in the US, Black Lives Matter is a global network of activists who demonstrate against police brutality and racially motivated acts of violence. After African American George Floyd was killed in police custody in May 2020, millions of people worldwide participated in Black Lives Matter protests to demand change.

Harlem Renaissance
An African American *cultural* movement based in Harlem, New York, US, that happened in the 1920s.

humanitarian
Someone who works to help improve human welfare.

Islamic world
A term for the countries where Islam is the main religion. It includes parts of North Africa, the Middle East, and Asia.

Ku Klux Klan
A violent terrorist secret society that was set up in the US after the Civil War to oppose Black emancipation.

missionary
A religious person who seeks to persuade others, often living in foreign lands, to adopt his or her religion.

monarchy
A type of government in which a king or queen is recognized as head of state, even though he or she may have no real political power.

morality
Beliefs based on the principles of what is right and wrong.

Muslim
A follower of Islam.

nation
An independent country, or one or more countries whose people share historical, linguistic, or cultural (see *culture*) ties.

Nobel Prize
Any of six international awards given annually for outstanding work in physics, chemistry, medicine, literature, economics, or the promotion of peace.

peace treaty
An official, written agreement between warring parties to bring hostilities to an end.

pilgrimage
A religious journey a person makes to a holy place.

pioneer
A person who is the first or among the first to do something important.

racism
Prejudice or discrimination directed against a person or people of a different race based on the belief that one's own race is superior.

republic
A country without a hereditary monarch (see *monarchy*) or *emperor*. Modern republics are usually headed by presidents.

revolt
An organized uprising intended to overthrow whoever is in authority.

revolution
A sudden and fundamental change in society brought about by an organized group of protesters.

Scramble for Africa
The invasion, occupation, division, and *colonization* of Africa by European powers between 1881 and 1914.

segregation
Separation, particularly of one race from another within a racist social system.

siege
To surround and blockade a city or fortress with the intention of capturing it.

sovereign
A ruler or head of state exerting supreme power.

treason
The crime of betraying one's country.

Underground Railroad
A network of secret routes and safe houses organized by Black and white anti-slavery activists in the US. Its aim was to help *enslaved people* escape from slavery to freedom.

United Nations
An international organization of countries set up in 1945 that aims to promote peace, security, and cooperation between its members.

West, the
Europe and North America or their ideals when seen in contrast to other civilizations.

Index

Page numbers in bold indicate main entries.

Acknowledgments

The publisher would like to thank the following for their assistance in the preparation of this book:
Additional writing: Amanda Wyatt. Editorial assistance and Index: Tayabah Khan. Jackets Editorial Coordinator: Priyanka Sharma. Managing Jackets Editor: Saloni Singh. Picture Researcher: Rituraj Singh. Assistant Picture Research Administrator: Vagisha Pushp. DTP Designer: Syed Md Farhan.

Some material in this book was previously published in *Timelines of Everything* (2018) and *Timelines of Everyone* (2020)

TIMELINES OF EVERYTHING
DK LONDON
Senior Art Editor Smiljka Surla
Senior Editor Sam Atkinson
Project Editors Steven Carton, Ben Ffrancon Davies, Sarah Edwards, Sarah MacLeod, Ben Morgan, Sophie Parkes, Laura Sandford, Pauline Savage, Amanda Wyatt
Project Designers Sunita Gahir, Alex Lloyd, Gregory McCarthy, Stefan Podhorodecki, Michelle Staples, Jacqui Swan, Sadie Thomas
Illustrators Acute Graphics, Peter Bull, Edwood Burn, Sunita Gahir, Clare Joyce, KJA Artists, Arran Lewis, Alex Lloyd, Maltings Partnership, Gus Scott
Picture Researchers Sarah Hopper, Jo Walton
Producers, Pre-Production David Almond, Andy Hilliard
Senior Producers Alex Bell, Mary Slater
Jacket Designers Surabhi Wadhwa-Gandhi, Juhi Sheth, Smiljka Surla
Jackets Editor Amelia Collins
Design Director Phil Ormerod
Contributors Laura Buller, Peter Chrisp, Alexander Cox, Susan Kennedy, Andrea Mills, Sally Regan

DK Delhi
DTP Designers Jaypal Singh Chauhan, Syed Mohammed Farhan
Senior DTP Designers Neeraj Bhatia, Jagtar Singh
Jackets Designer Juhi Sheth
Jacket Senior DTP Designer Harish Aggarwal
Jacket DTP Designer Rakesh Kumar
Jackets Editorial Coordinator Priyanka Sharma
Managing Jackets Editor Saloni Singh

TIMELINES OF EVERYONE
DK LONDON
Senior Editor Steven Carton
Senior Art Editor Smiljka Surla
Project Editors Edward Aves, Thomas Booth
Project Designers Sunita Gahir, Joe Lawrence, Jessica Tapolcai
Editors Ben Ffrancon Davies, Tayabah Khan
Design Assistants Naomi Murray, Lauren Quinn
Illustrators Peter Bull Art Studio, Gary Bullock Illustration, Barry Croucher/The Art Agency, Rob Davis/The Art Agency, Sunita Gahir, Peter Johnston/The Art Agency, Naomi Murray, Lauren Quinn, Claudia Saraceni/The Art Agency, Gus Scott, Peter David Scott/The Art Agency
Senior Picture Researcher Myriam Megharbi
Production Editor Gillian Reid
Senior Producer Meskerem Berhane

Jacket Designer Surabhi Wadhwa-Gandhi
Contributors A. M. Dassu, Mireille Harper, Lisa Sade Kennedy, Susan Kennedy, Francesca Kletz, Sally Regan

DK DELHI
Jacket Designer Tanya Mehrotra
Senior Picture Researcher Taiyaba Khatoon
Senior Picture Researcher Surya Sankash Sarangi
Assistant Picture Researcher Vagisha Pushp

For both books:
DK Media Archive Romaine Werblow
Managing Editor Lisa Gillespie
Managing Art Editor Owen Peyton Jones
Jackets Design Development Manager Sophia MTT
Publisher Andrew Macintyre
Art Director Karen Self
Associate Publishing Director Liz Wheeler
Publishing Director Jonathan Metcalf
Consultant Philip Parker

PILL 22-01-21

PILL 22-01-21